ANTISOCIAL BEHAVIOUR LE

ANTISOCIAL BEHAVIOUR LEGISLATION

Annotated by

Tom Guthrie

Senior Lecturer, University of Glasgow

THOMSON

W. GREEN

Published in 2005 by

W. Green & Son Ltd
21 Alva Street
Edinburgh EH2 4PS

www.wgreen.thomson.com

Typeset by LBJ Typesetting Ltd of Kingsclere

Printed in and bound in Great Britain by
Athenaeum Press Ltd, Gateshead, Tyne & Weir

No natural forests were destroyed to make this product;
Only farmed timber was used and replanted

A CIP catalogue record for this book is available from the British Library

ISBN 0 414 016 270

CONTENTS

TABLE OF CASES

TABLE OF STATUTES

Table of Statutes

TABLE OF STATUTORY INSTRUMENTS

Table of Statutory Instruments

PART A—THE ACT

ANTISOCIAL BEHAVIOUR ETC. (SCOTLAND) ACT 2004

(asp 8)

CONTENTS

PART 1

ANTISOCIAL BEHAVIOUR STRATEGIES

PART 2

ANTISOCIAL BEHAVIOUR ORDERS

Antisocial behaviour orders

Interim antisocial behaviour orders

Notification of orders

Breach of orders

Orders in respect of children

Provision of information and records

Guidance and research

Interpretation

1

PART 3

DISPERSAL OF GROUPS

Authorisations and powers

Guidance and research

Interpretation

PART 4

CLOSURE OF PREMISES

Closure notices

Closure orders

General

Interpretation

PART 5

NOISE NUISANCE

Summary procedure for dealing with noise from certain places

Noise control provisions

PART 6

THE ENVIRONMENT

Controlled waste and litter

Graffiti

Penalties for environmental offences

Interpretation

PART 7

HOUSING: ANTISOCIAL BEHAVIOUR NOTICES

Antisocial behaviour notices

Failure to comply with notice: sanctions

PART 8

HOUSING: REGISTRATION OF CERTAIN LANDLORDS

Registration

Enforcement

Grants

Regulations

Amendment of Housing (Scotland) Act 1988

Interpretation

PART 9

PARENTING ORDERS

Applications

The Bill for this Act of the Scottish Parliament was passed by the Parliament on 17th June 2004 and received Royal Assent on 26th July 2004

An Act of the Scottish Parliament to make provision in connection with antisocial behaviour; to make provision about criminal justice; to make provision in relation to child welfare; and for connected purposes.

Introduction and General Note
The various provisions contained in Antisocial Behaviour etc. (Scotland) Act 2004 (asp 8) ("this Act") were first proposed in a consultation paper, *Putting our communities first: A*

Strategy for tackling Anti-social Behaviour (Scottish Executive Edinburgh 2003). This was designed to set out a policy for dealing with the perceived problems of antisocial behaviour or 'ned culture'. The proposals involved a mixture of extension of existing provision, for example extending antisocial behaviour orders to children aged 12 or over, new provisions reflecting developments in England and Wales, for example police powers to disperse groups, and other new provisions, for example a requirement for all landlords to register with a local authority. The responses to the consultation were mixed, with some of the proposals attracting significant opposition, for example the dispersal powers. Despite the opposition, many of the proposals made their way into the Act and through the Parliament largely unchanged. The responses are analysed in Flint J, Atkinson R, and Scott S, *A Report on the Consultation Responses to Putting Our Communities First* (Department id Urban Studies, University of Glasgow, October 2003) available at: http://www.scotland.gov.uk/library5/social/stabmr.pdf.

Two of the areas of concern which remained in place throughout the passing of the Act were the relationship between various measures contained in the Act for dealing with children under 16 and the existing children's hearing system and the compatibility of some of the powers with the European Convention on Human Rights.

Since the implementation of the Social Work (Scotland) Act 1968 (c.49) children under the age of 16 who commit offences or whose behaviour might be classified as antisocial have, for the most part been dealt with by the children's hearing system. The emphasis in the system is on addressing the needs of the child and his/her family rather than on punishment of the child. The provisions in this Act mark a move away from this type of philosophy towards, at least as regards some children, a more punitive approach. One example is the extension of Antisocial Behaviour Orders to children aged 12 or over. Although a children's hearing will be involved in giving advice to the sheriff making the order (s.4(4)), there is no requirement for the sheriff to follow that advice nor, if an order is made, is there a requirement that the type of support available when a supervision requirement in respect of a child is made by a children's hearing will be made available to the child.

In the General Notes on each section reference is made, where appropriate, to possible inconsistencies with the European Convention on Human Rights, for a more general survey see Ashworth, A, 'Social Control and "Anti-Social Behaviour": The Subversion of Human Rights?', (2004) 120 *Law Quarterly Review*, 263. Aside from Arts 5 and 6 which are largely concerned with procedural matters, the other convention rights which may be affected are those conferred by Art.8 (private and family life, may be relevant, for example in the context of parenting orders) and Art.11 (peaceful assembly, may be engaged in relation to powers to disperse groups). An important point to be borne in mind is that although the Scottish Executive and the courts may be satisfied that the legislation is compliant with the European Convention there will also be an issue in each individual case as to whether any infringement of the rights of an individual is justified as a proportionate intervention designed to achieve objectives designated as permissible in the Convention.

Structure of the Act
This is as follows:
Part 1 deals with antisocial behaviour strategies.
Part 2 is concerned with antisocial behaviour orders and replaces the previous provisions in the Crime and Disorder Act 1998 (c.37).
Part 3 sets out the new police powers to disperse groups and the circumstances in which they can be exercised.
Part 4 contains provision for the compulsory closure of premises which are connected to antisocial behaviour.
Part 5 introduces new controls on noise nuisance, supplementing existing legislation.
Part 6 is concerned with the environment and makes slight alterations to existing legislation on litter and waste disposal as well as introducing new powers to require the removal of graffiti.
Part 7 gives local authorities the power to serve a notice on landlords requiring them to take action to stop antisocial behaviour by their tenants.
Part 8 introduces a compulsory register for landlords in the private sector.
Part 9 contains provisions for the making of parenting orders.
Part 10 is concerned with the powers of criminal courts, they are given the power to make an anti-social behaviour order on conviction, a new penalty, the community reparation order, is introduced, the lower age limit of 16 is removed in respect of restriction of liberty orders, opening them up to any child being dealt with in the criminal court system, an offence of

selling spray paint to children is introduced, as are powers to seize vehicles which are being or have been used in an antisocial manner.

Part 11 introduces fixed penalty notices for a range of offences involving antisocial behaviour. Part 12 contains provisions relating to the children's hearing system and imposing a duty on local authorities to comply with their duties in respect of supervision requirements made by hearings.

Part 13 contains definitions and provisions for the sharing of information.

Guidance

There is a large amount of guidance accompanying this Act, it is available as follows:

Guidance on Antisocial Behaviour Strategies: http://www.scotland.gov.uk/library5/social/asbs2.pdf

Guidance on Antisocial Behaviour Orders: http://www.scotland.gov.uk/library5/social/asbsg.pdf

Guidance on Dispersal of Groups: http://www.scotland.gov.uk/library5/social/asbd.pdf.

Guidance on Closure of Premises: http://www.scotland.gov.uk/library5/social/asbcp.pdf

Guidance on Noise Nuisance: http://www.scotland.gov.uk/library5/social/asbn.pdf.

Guidance on Ban on Sale of Spray Paint to Under 16s: http://www.scotland.gov.uk/library5/social/asbp.pdf

Guidance on Graffiti Removal: http://www.scotland.gov.uk/library5/social/asbgr.pdf

Guidance on Disclosure and Sharing of Information: http://www.scotland.gov.uk/library5/social/asbi.pdf

Guidance on Local Authority Accountability: http://www.scotland.gov.uk/library5/localgov/laaasb.pdf.

Guidance on Parenting Orders: http://www.scotland.gov.uk/Resource/Doc/37432/0011355.pdf

With the exception of the last two of these (all last accessed on June 27, 2005) these are also available on the Executive's Antisocial Behaviour website, which also contains a variety of other information: http://www.antisocialbehaviourscotland.com

COMMENCEMENT

Parts 1, 3, 4 and 11 came into effect on October 28, 2004, as did ss.4–12, 14–18, 56–67, 100, 118–119, 120, 126–127 (though the relevant regulations will not be made until early in 2005), 138–140, 142 and 143. The following provisions came into effect on November 5, 2004: ss.55, 122–125, Pt 5. The following provisions came into effect on January 31, 2005: ss.135–137. The following provisions came into effect on April 4, 2005: ss.13, 98, 121 and Pt 9. All brought into force by the Antisocial Behaviour etc. (Scotland) Act 2004 (Commencement and Savings) Order 2004 (SSI 2004/420). Parts 7 and 8 are scheduled to come into effect in November 2005.

ABBREVIATIONS

"this Act":   Antisocial Behaviour etc. (Scotland) Act 2004 (asp 8)

PART 1

ANTISOCIAL BEHAVIOUR STRATEGIES

Antisocial behaviour strategies
1.—(1) Each local authority and relevant chief constable shall, acting jointly, prepare a strategy for dealing with antisocial behaviour in the authority's area.(2) Each local authority shall publish the strategy.(3) The strategy shall in particular—
  (a) set out an assessment of the extent of occurrences of antisocial behaviour in the authority's area;
  (b) set out an assessment of the types of antisocial behaviour occurring in the authority's area;
  (c) specify arrangements for consulting community bodies and other persons (including in particular young persons) in each part of the authority's area in which there are (or are likely to be) occurrences of antisocial behaviour, about how to deal with antisocial behaviour in the part;
  (d) specify the range and availability in the authority's area of any services—
      (i) for persons under the age of 16 years; and
      (ii) for persons generally,
which are designed to deal with antisocial behaviour occurring there, the consequences of such behaviour or the prevention of such behaviour;
  (e) in so far as not specified under paragraph (d), specify the range and availability in the authority's area of any services for—
      (i) victims of antisocial behaviour;
      (ii) persons who witness occurrences of antisocial behaviour; and
      (iii) the provision of mediation in relation to disputes arising from antisocial behaviour; and
  (f) make provision about—
      (i) how the authority and the relevant chief constable are to co-ordinate the discharge of their functions in so far as they may be discharged in relation to antisocial behaviour in the authority's area;
      (ii) the exchange of information relating to such behaviour between the authority and the relevant chief constable;
      (iii) the giving by the authority and the relevant chief constable of information of that kind to such other persons as appear to the authority and the chief constable to have an interest in dealing with antisocial behaviour and the receipt by the authority and the chief constable of information of that kind from those other persons; and
      (iv) the exchange of information relating to antisocial behaviour among such other persons as are mentioned in sub-paragraph (iii).
(4) The local authority and the relevant chief constable—
  (a) shall keep the strategy under review; and
  (b) may from time to time revise the strategy.
(5) If a strategy is revised under subsection (4), the local authority shall publish the revised strategy.
(6) In preparing, reviewing and revising the strategy, the local authority shall consult—

(a) the Principal Reporter;
(b) registered social landlords which provide or manage property in the authority's area; and
(c) such community bodies and other persons as the local authority considers appropriate.

(7) In considering which persons to consult, the local authority shall seek to include those who are representative of persons adversely affected by antisocial behaviour.

(8) Each local authority and relevant chief constable shall, in discharging functions under this section and in implementing a strategy as published under it, have regard to any guidance issued by the Scottish Ministers about those matters.

(9) Before issuing any such guidance, the Scottish Ministers shall consult such persons as they see fit.

(10) For the purposes of subsection (1), the Scottish Ministers may by directions require such persons as appear to them to hold information relating to antisocial behaviour to supply—
(a) such information as may be specified in the direction; or
(b) information of a description specified in the direction,
to a local authority and relevant chief constable.

(11) In this section—

"community bodies" has the meaning given by section 15(4) of the Local Government in Scotland Act 2003 (asp 1); and
"relevant chief constable", in relation to a local authority, means the chief constable for the police area which is wholly or partly within the area of the authority.

DEFINITIONS
"community bodies":   subs.(11)
"relevant chief constable":   subs.(11)
"antisocial behaviour":   s.143
"registered social landlord":   Housing (Scotland) Act 2001(asp 10), s.57

GENERAL NOTE
Acting together local authorities and chief constable are required to prepare an Antisocial Behaviour Strategy for the area of the local authority. It is suggested that this will be done using community planning processes and structures (*Guidance on Antisocial Behaviour Strategies*, paras 5, 16–19. The contents of the strategy are set out in subs.(3), to which can be added a requirement to set out the overall aims or outcomes of the strategy as well as setting out a timescale for achieving certain objectives which contribute towards these overall outcomes (*Guidance on Antisocial Behaviour Strategies*, para.81). The strategy must be kept under review, and there must be consultation both in the setting of the original strategy and any review. The groups to be consulted are set out in subss (6) and (7), the latter emphasising the need to involve victims of antisocial behaviour. Private sector housing organisations will also need to be involved if these are significant in the area, as will local business organisations (*Guidance on Antisocial Behaviour Strategies*, paras 53–54). The guidance makes it clear that consultation is not to be just a one off event, but rather a continuing process of engagement with groups such as community councils, youth groups and through community planning structures (*Guidance on Antisocial Behaviour Strategies*, paras 57–61). The guidance also stresses the need to integrate this strategy with other local authority strategies (listing ten of these).

Reports and information
2.—(1) Subject to subsection (3)(b), each local authority shall from time to time publish reports on—
(a) how the authority and the relevant chief constable have implemented the strategy as published under section 1(2) or (5); and
(b) what were the results of that implementation.
(2) It shall be the duty of—
(a) the relevant chief constable;
(b) the Principal Reporter; and
(c) any registered social landlord which provides or manages property within the area of the local authority that published the strategy,
to provide such information as the authority may reasonably require in order to enable the authority to comply with the duty under subsection (1).
(3) The Scottish Ministers may by regulations make provision as to—
(a) the form and content of reports under subsection (1); and
(b) the frequency and timing of publication of such reports.
(4) Before making regulations under subsection (3) the Scottish Ministers shall consult—
(a) such associations of local authorities; and
(b) such other persons,
as they think fit.
(5) A local authority shall, on being so required by the Scottish Ministers, provide them with reports or other information (being reports or information about the matters referred to in subsection (1)) of such kind as they specify in the requirement.
(6) In this section "relevant chief constable" has the same meaning as in section 1.

DEFINITIONS
"relevant chief constable":   s.1(11)
"registered social landlord":   Housing (Scotland) Act 2001, s.57

GENERAL NOTE
There is a duty to report on implementation of the Antisocial Behaviour Strategy and the results of that implementation. The frequency of report and the contents of the report are still to be specified.

Scottish Ministers' power to apply sections 1 and 2 to registered social landlords
3.—(1) The Scottish Ministers may make regulations for the purpose of securing the participation of a registered social landlord in the preparation, review or revision of a strategy such as is mentioned in section 1(1).
(2) Regulations under subsection (1) may in particular make such modifications of sections 1(1), (3), (4), (6) and (8) and 2(1) as the Scottish Ministers consider necessary or expedient for that purpose.

DEFINITIONS
"registered social landlord":   Housing (Scotland) Act 2001, s.57

GENERAL NOTE
This section envisages a requirement to involve registered social landlords as principals rather than merely as consultees in the preparation of Antisocial Behaviour Strategies. This may be appropriate where either a large part of the housing stock in an authority is managed by registered social landlords or the areas affected by antisocial behaviour are so managed.

PART 2

ANTISOCIAL BEHAVIOUR ORDERS

Antisocial behaviour orders

Antisocial behaviour orders

4.—(1) On the application of a relevant authority, the sheriff may, if satisfied that the conditions mentioned in subsection (2) are met as respects the person to whom the application relates (the "specified person"), make an antisocial behaviour order.

(2) Those conditions are—

(a) that the specified person is at least 12 years of age;

(b) that the specified person has engaged in antisocial behaviour towards a relevant person; and

(c) that an antisocial behaviour order is necessary for the purpose of protecting relevant persons from further antisocial behaviour by the specified person.

(3) For the purpose of determining whether the condition mentioned in subsection (2)(b) is met, the sheriff shall disregard any act or conduct of the specified person which that person shows was reasonable in the circumstances.

(4) Where the specified person is a child, the sheriff shall, before determining the application, require the Principal Reporter to arrange a children's hearing for the purpose of obtaining their advice as to whether the condition mentioned in subsection (2)(c) is met; and the sheriff shall, in determining whether that condition is met, have regard to that advice.

(5) Subject to subsections (6) and (7), an antisocial behaviour order is an order which prohibits, indefinitely or for such period as may be specified in the order, the specified person from doing anything described in the order.

(6) The prohibitions that may be imposed by an antisocial behaviour order are those necessary for the purpose of protecting relevant persons from further antisocial behaviour by the specified person.

(7) If an antisocial behaviour order is made on the application of a local authority the order may, in addition to imposing prohibitions that are necessary for the purpose mentioned in subsection (6), impose such prohibitions as are necessary for the purpose of protecting other persons ("affected persons") from further antisocial behaviour by the specified person.

(8) Before making an antisocial behaviour order, the sheriff shall, where the specified person is present in court, explain in ordinary language—

(a) the effect of the order and the prohibitions proposed to be included in it;

(b) the consequences of failing to comply with the order;

(c) the powers the sheriff has under sections 5 and 6; and

(d) the entitlement of the specified person to appeal against the making of the order.

(9) Failure to comply with subsection (8) shall not affect the validity of the order.

(10) An application for an antisocial behaviour order shall be made by summary application to the sheriff within whose sheriffdom the specified person is alleged to have engaged in antisocial behaviour.

(11) Before making an application under this section—

(a) a relevant authority shall consult the relevant consultees; and

(b) a registered social landlord shall—

(i) in the case where the specified person is a child, consult the local authority within whose area the specified person resides or appears to reside about the proposed application;

(ii) in the case where the specified person is not a child, notify that local authority of the proposed application.

(12) Nothing in this section shall prevent a relevant authority from instituting any legal proceedings otherwise than under this section against any person in relation to any antisocial behaviour.

(13) In this section, "relevant person" means—

(a) in relation to an application by a local authority, a person within the area of the authority; and

(b) in relation to an application by a registered social landlord—

(i) a person residing in, or otherwise in or likely to be in, property provided or managed by that landlord; or

(ii) a person in, or likely to be in, the vicinity of such property.

DEFINITIONS

"antisocial behaviour":	s.143
"antisocial behaviour order":	subs.(4)
"specified person":	subs.(3)
"relevant authority":	s.15
"relevant person":	subs.(1)
"relevant consultees":	s.15

GENERAL NOTE

This section essentially repeats the provisions previously contained in ss.19–21 of the Crime and Disorder Act 1998, as amended by the Criminal Justice (Scotland) Act 2003, s.44 (adding interim orders). There is one significant, and during the passing of this Act, controversial addition, that is the extension of antisocial behaviour orders to children aged 12 or over, the previous lower age limit being 16. The rationale for this extension was to 'deal with a small number of persistently difficult young people for whom the hearings system has not proved effective in changing behaviour' (*per* the Minister for Communities (Margaret Curran), Official Report, June 17, 2004, col.9169). Extension of the availability of these orders has certain knock on consequences. One of these is the possibility of a parenting order being made at the same time as an ASBO (s.13). A second consequence will apply where the child's family are tenants of a registered social landlord. The legislation governing such tenancies (the Housing (Scotland) Act 2001 (asp 10)) allows the landlord to convert a tenancy of accommodation rented from them from a Scottish secure tenancy to a short Scottish secure tenancy on the making of an ASBO against the tenant or anyone living with them (Housing (Scotland) Act 2001, s.21). Clearly this provision will be available where an ASBO is made against a child of the tenant aged between 12 and 15. In addition, where an ASBO has been made against a prospective tenant or someone residing with them, the landlord can offer a short Scottish secure tenancy. The security of tenure for a tenant holding on a short Scottish secure tenancy is less than that of a Scottish secure tenant. The *Guidance on Antisocial Behaviour Orders* suggests that conversion to a short Scottish secure tenancy should only take place where the antisocial behaviour underlying the ASBO is related to the tenancy, or example taking place in or close to the rented property (paras 132–134). Finally, an ASBO made against a child aged 12–15 will, in the same way as an order made against an adult, affect the rights of the family if they become homeless (Housing (Scotland) Act 1987 (c.26), s.2C)

The making of an order has a potential effect on rights under Articles 8 (right to a family life) and 11 (assembly) amongst others. For a discussion of potential problems see Reid, K, 'Anti-social behaviour orders: some current issues', (2002) 24 JSWFL, 205 at 214–216.

An alternative to considering an ASBO would be to make an Acceptable Behaviour Contract with the individual whose behaviour was giving cause for concern. This could be either as an alternative to an ASBO or it might be made clear in the Contract that failure to keep to it would result in an application being made for an ASBO. See *Guidance on Antisocial Behaviour Orders*, paras 49–53, Bullock K and Jones B, *Acceptable Behaviour Contracts addressing antisocial behaviour in the London Borough of Islington* (2004), Home Office Online Report 02/04, available at: http://www.homeoffice.gov.uk/rds/pdfs2/rdsolr0204.pdf) Although Acceptable Behaviour Contracts are seen as an important part of the process of dealing with antisocial behaviour there is as yet no specific Scottish guidance on these (for guidance in

England and Wales see: Home Office/Youth Justice Board/ACPO, *A Guide to Anti-Social Behaviour Orders and Acceptable Behaviour Contracts* available at: http://www.crimereduction.gov.uk/asbos9.pdf; see also *Guidance on Antisocial Behaviour Orders, paras. 49–53).*

What is antisocial behaviour?
This is considered more fully in the general note to s.143. At this stage the broad scope of the definition should be noted, it covers not only what might immediately spring to mind as antisocial behaviour, but has also proved itself open to innovative use, for example orders taken out against the operators of flyposting businesses. In addition, neither the definition nor the grounds set out in subs.(2) make any reference to the intentionality of the behaviour, the degree of control the person has over the behaviour, or their appreciation that it is antisocial. These omissions in the Bill raised concerns about possible inappropriate use of ASBOs against persons with, for example, an autistic spectrum disorder or a learning disability. As discussed in the general note to s.143 and below under consideration of the grounds for granting an order, these issues are dealt with in the guidance issued by the Scottish Executive.

Before an order is applied for
Subsection (11) sets out the list of those who must be consulted before an application for an ASBO is made. The *Guidance on Antisocial Behaviour Orders* contains more detail on the processes to be gone through before an application is made. This requires that each authority develop a policy setting out the circumstances in which an order might be applied for, as well as emphasising the need for strong evidence and the need to consider whether an ASBO is the most appropriate remedy in the circumstances. Consideration of this last point will include consideration of the appropriateness of this remedy in respect of the person against whom the order is sought in light, for example, of any disability affecting them.

The grounds for granting an order
As well as the age requirement, the sheriff must be satisfied that there has been antisocial behaviour and that an order is necessary to protect from further antisocial behaviour. The antisocial behaviour must have affected a 'relevant person'. Where the application is made by a local authority this includes anyone within the local authority's boundaries, though they need not be resident there. Where the applicant is a registered social landlord a relevant person will be either someone residing in or otherwise in accommodation managed by them or someone in the vicinity of such property. Because of this it is unlikely that a registered social landlord could obtain an ASBO in order to protect an owner occupier (who had, for example exercised their right to buy) living amongst tenants of the landlord, (see *Manchester City Council v Lee* [2003] EWCA Civ 1256). Because all of these limits apply only to the victims of antisocial behaviour the person who will be subject to the order does not need to fall into any of these categories.
There is a defence that in deciding whether there has been antisocial behaviour any behaviour which is reasonable in the circumstances should be excluded from consideration (subs.(3)). This defence might be available where the behaviour complained about is the result of a learning disability or other condition that affects an individual's behaviour. This is not clearly spelled out in the legislation, however, nor is it a requirement that the behaviour be intentional. Where the behaviour is not intentional or is the product of a disability or condition it will, of course, be possible to argue that the final condition is not met. Making an order in these circumstances, is, without other forms of support, unlikely to be an effective means of preventing future conduct.
The position of someone who cannot understand the consequences of their actions is addressed more fully in the *Guidance on Antisocial Behaviour Orders* (at para.28). This suggests that it is unlikely that an ASBO will be appropriate in such cases, encouraging authorities not to apply for an order in the first place. In addition, s.140 requires anyone discharging a function under the Act to do so in a manner that encourages equal opportunities. As defined in the Scotland Act 1998 (c.46) (Section L2 of Pt II of Sch.5) 'equal opportunities' includes 'the prevention, elimination or regulation of discrimination between persons on grounds of . . . of disability.' Inappropriate action against individuals whose behaviour flows from their disability would be inconsistent with this.

Children under 16
Additional consultations are required before an order in respect of a child is applied for (s.18) and subs.(4), introduced to ally fears that orders would routinely be used against this

age group, requires the sheriff to seek the views of a children's hearing before an order (but not an interim order, see s.7) is made. The specific remit of the hearing is to consider whether the making of an order is necessary. The *Guidance on Antisocial Behaviour Orders* devotes considerable space to use of ASBOs against this age group (paras 54–69) and concludes that these are only intended to deal with 'a small number of persistently antisocial young people for whom alternatives available are not working' (para.64). Although the guidance does not deal with the issue specifically, it will also be relevant to consider whether the child is looked after by the local authority. If he/she is, then the provisions of s.17 of the Children (Scotland) Act 1995 (c.36) will come into play. This requires both that the authority promote and safeguard the welfare of the child and that extensive consultations take place before decisions are made in respect of the child. There is a potential conflict of interest for local authorities in cases where consideration is being given to applying for an ASBO for a child being looked after, and it will be essential for the authority to ensure that its obligations in respect of promoting welfare and with regard to consultation are fulfilled (see the discussion in *R. (on the application of M (A Child)) v Sheffield Magistrates Court* [2004] EWHC 1830), where it was held that a decision to apply for an ASBO was a decision to which the consultation duty applied and where guidance was given on the processes to be followed and the support to be offered to the child during this process). The duty to consult under s.17, at least as regards the parents is consistent with the case law of the European Court of Human Rights in respect of the rights to consultation involved in Article 8 of the European Convention on Human Rights (see, for example, *R v United Kingdom* [1988] 2 F.L.R. 445). In contrast, it is not necessary to carry out any process of consultation involving the person who may be subject to an ASBO before application is made for an order against an adult (*Wareham v Purbreck District Council* [2005] EWHC 358 (Admin), considering whether this was required by Art. 8 of the European Convention on Human Rights.).

The duty to promote the welfare of the child under s.17 is not, of course, absolute. Local authorities are permitted to depart from this where it is necessary "for the purpose of protecting members of the public from serious harm (whether or not physical harm)" (s.17(5)). This is a high standard and, from the definition of antisocial behaviour set out in s.143 it will be clear that most instances of it will not involve protecting the public from *serious* harm.

Similar issues might arise where the child falls within the definition of a child in need under the Children (Scotland) Act 1995, s.22 of which imposes on a local authority an obligation to safeguard and promote the welfare of children in this category. The impact of this will be less than in relation to children looked after, particularly if, as has been the case in England, this is viewed simply as a target duty (as, for example, in *R. (on the application of G) v Barnet LBC* [2004] 2 AC 208).

Standard of Proof

In *R. (on the application of McCann) v Manchester Crown Court* [2003] 1 AC 787 the House of Lords decided by that the application for an ASBO is a civil proceeding (though see the criticism of this in Ashworth, A, 'Social Control and "Anti-Social Behaviour"': The Subversion of Human Rights?', (2004) 120 *Law Quarterly Review* 263). Despite this, they also held that the standard of proof for establishing the antisocial behaviour on which the application for an ASBO is based is proof beyond a reasonable doubt. This will cover both the conduct *per se* and establishing its effect or likely effect on others. Although this is an English decision, the logic of the opinion of Lord Hope is that the same conclusion would be reached in Scotland. (see also *Chief Constable of Lancashire v Potter* [2003] EWHC 2272; *Glasgow Housing Association v John O'Donnell*, Sheriff Holligan, Glasgow Sheriff Court, August 4, 2004 (available at www.scotcourts.gov.uk); *Glasgow Housing Association v David Sharkey*, 2005 S.L.T. (Sh Ct) 59. Although the standard of proof is criminal the evidence available to establish this will include, as the proceedings are civil, hearsay evidence.

As regards subs.(2)(c), the suggestion in *McCann* is that this does not involve a standard of proof, but rather involves an exercise of judgement or evaluation (*per* Lord Steyn at para.37). See General Note to s.7 for a discussion of necessity.

Prohibitions in an ASBO

The actions prohibited in an ASBO need not be in themselves criminal, and there is a variety of instances of this, for example restrictions on entering certain areas and, notoriously, a restriction on a woman answering her front door in her underwear (see http://

www.timesonline.co.uk/article/0,,2090–1513243,00.html). It is clear that the prohibitions must prevent certain behaviour rather than clearly requiring some positive action on the part of the person subject to the order (in other words a mandatory requirement). See the discussion in *Lonergan v Lewes Crown Court* [2005] EWHC 457 (Admin), the example given in *The Queen (on the application of M) v Sheffield Magistrates Court* ([2004] EWHC 1830 (Admin) (at para.57) is of an order prohibiting residence anywhere but at a single address, which is effectively a mandatory order to stay at that address.

Prohibitions included in an order can be for the whole duration of the order or for a shorter period, for example curfew provisions might be for a shorter duration (*Lonergan v Lewes Crown Court* [2005] EWHC 457 (Admin)).

The effect of an ASBO

The ASBO can only contain requirements in the form of prohibitions, and there is no provision for any support or other intervention to challenge the underlying behaviour. Although an application made by a local authority must be based on antisocial behaviour directed against people within its area, the prohibitions in the order can be directed to protecting people who do not fall into this category, so in principle the order can extend beyond the geographical limits of the particular local authority. Where the application is made by a registered social landlord the scope of the prohibitions is more limited and is essentially tied to property that they manage. The granting of an order does not prevent other action based on the same antisocial behaviour, for example eviction proceedings.

The length of the order should be indicated in the application, though it is possible to have an order without limit of time. Although there is no statutory requirement for review, the *Guidance on Antisocial Behaviour Orders* indicates that these should be reviewed by the local authority or registered social landlord at least every six months and that consideration should be given to revocation at least annually (para.126)

It has also been held that in appropriate circumstance a local authority or registered social landlord is entitled to publicise details of ASBOs, including photographs of individuals against whom orders have been granted (*R. (on the application of Stanley) v Commissioner of Police of the Metropolis* [2004] EWHC 2229).

Antisocial behaviour orders: variation and revocation

5.—(1) On the application of—

(a) the relevant authority that obtained an antisocial behaviour order; or

(b) the person subject to such an order,

the sheriff may vary or revoke the order.

(2) Where the person subject to the order is a child, the sheriff shall, in determining whether to vary or revoke it, have regard to any views expressed by the Principal Reporter.

(3) Before making an application under this section—

(a) a relevant authority shall consult the relevant consultees; and

(b) a registered social landlord shall—

(i) in the case where the person subject to the order is a child, consult the local authority within whose area the person resides or appears to reside about the proposed application;

(ii) in the case where the person subject to the order is not a child, notify that local authority of the proposed application.

DEFINITIONS

"antisocial behaviour order":   s.4(4)

"relevant authority":   s.15

"registered social landlord":   Housing (Scotland) Act 2001, s.57

GENERAL NOTE

This section allows applications for variation or revocation of an order to be made either by the local authority or registered social landlord which obtained the order or the person who is subject to the order. If the application is made by either of the first two then certain consultations, set out in subs.(3) are necessary. This section should be read together with the guidance on review of orders in the *Guidance on Antisocial Behaviour Orders* (paras 125–6). Where the person subject to the order is under the age of 16 the views of the Principal Reporter have to be taken into account.

The ability to seek revocation or alteration is restricted by s.6, which indicates that an individual cannot make an application under this section pending the resolution of an appeal by them against either the granting or the variation of an order.

Appeals: effect on competence of application under section 5

6. Where a person appeals against—

(a) the making of an antisocial behaviour order; or

(b) the variation, under section 5, of such an order,

it shall not be competent for that person to make an application under that section before the appeal is disposed of or abandoned.

DEFINITIONS

"antisocial behaviour order": s.4(4)

GENERAL NOTE

See General Note to s.5.

Interim antisocial behaviour orders

Interim antisocial behaviour orders

7. (1) Subsection (2) applies where—

(a) an application is made under section 4; and

(b) the application has been intimated to the specified person.

(2) If the sheriff is satisfied—

(a) that the condition mentioned in paragraph (a) of section 4(2) is met;

(b) that *prima facie* the condition mentioned in paragraph (b) of that section is met; and

(c) that the making of an interim antisocial behaviour order (an "interim order") is necessary for the purpose mentioned in paragraph (c) of that section,

the sheriff may make an interim order.

(3) Where the specified person is a child, the sheriff shall, in determining whether to make an interim order, have regard to any views expressed by the Principal Reporter.

(4) An interim order is an order which prohibits, pending the determination of the application, the specified person from doing anything described in the order.

(5) Sections 4(6) and (7) shall apply to an interim order as they apply to an antisocial behaviour order.

(6) Before making an interim order, the sheriff shall, where the specified person is present in court, explain in ordinary language—

(a) the effect of the order and the prohibitions proposed to be included in it;

(b) the consequences of failing to comply with the order;

(c) the power the sheriff has to recall the order; and

(d) the entitlement of the specified person to appeal against the making of the order.

(7) Failure to comply with subsection (6) shall not affect the validity of the order.

(8) An interlocutor granting or refusing an interim order is an appealable interlocutor.

DEFINITIONS
"specified person": s.4(3)

GENERAL NOTE

An application for an ASBO can contain a crave for the grant of an interim order, which will take effect pending the determination of the application for the full order. An application for an interim order can only be considered by the sheriff after the initial writ seeking an ASBO and asking for an interim order to be made has been intimated to the person against whom the order is sought (Rule 3.27.3 of Act of Sederunt (Summary Applications, Statutory Applications and Appeals etc. Rules) 1999 (SI 1999/929), as amended by the Act of Sederunt (Summary Applications, Statutory Applications and Appeals etc. Rules) Amendment (Antisocial Behaviour etc. (Scotland) Act 2004) 2004 (SSI 2004/455)).

The consistency of interim orders with Art.6 of the European Convention on Human Rights was considered in *R. (on the application of M) v Secretary of State for Constitutional Affairs* [2004] 2 All E.R. 531 where it was held that Art.6 was not engaged as the interim order was not determinative of civil rights and obligations because it was an interim order which could be brought back to court at any stage. Given the differences between the English provisions for interim orders and those above, for example, in the English context interim orders are for a fixed period and can be varied or discharged (Crime and Disorder Act 1998, s.1D) it is not necessarily the case that the same conclusion would be reached here. However, in that case it was also held that if Art.6 was engaged the procedure for the interim order was compliant. However, where, in an individual case, an interim order lasts for a considerable period of time, Art.6 may be engaged because the civil rights and obligations of the person will have been effectively determined by the interim order without proper and full consideration by a court. The question in such a case would be whether the right of appeal against the interim order would be sufficient to comply with Art.6.

Before an interim order can be made there is still an evidential burden on the applicant to establish a *prima facie* case that there has been antisocial behaviour and that the interim order is necessary to protect against future such behaviour. The first of these requirements requires that the sheriff is satisfied that if the conduct set out in the averments made in the application were established it would amount to antisocial behaviour. Whether or not the order is necessary is a matter for the sheriff's judgement. It has been suggested that in deciding this the allegations made in support of the application and whether these disclose serious public disorder will be relevant as well as the length of the likely delay before a proof hearing on the application for a full order and the position of the defender in relation to the allegations (*Glasgow Housing Association v David Sharkey*, 2005 S.L.T. (Sh Ct) 59; see also *Glasgow Housing Association v John O'Donnell*, Sheriff Holligan, Glasgow Sheriff Court, August 4, 2004, note also the comments on the use of affidavits and witness statements in applications in this second case).

There is also a requirement to obtain the views of the Principal Reporter in cases involving children. The sheriff cannot consider an application for an interim order against a child unless a written statement of these views has been lodged (Rule 3.27.3 of the Act of Sederunt (Summary Applications, Statutory Applications and Appeals etc. Rules) 1999 (SI 1999/929) added by the Act of Sederunt (Summary Applications, Statutory Applications and Appeals etc Rules) Amendment (Antisocial Behaviour etc. (Scotland) Act 2004), 2004 (SSI 2004/455)). The order can contain the same types of prohibition as a full order (subs.(5)). There is a right of appeal against the making of an interim order, either to the Sheriff Principal or direct to the Inner House of the Court of Session.

Notification of orders

Notification of making etc. of orders and interim orders

8.—(1) Subsection (2) applies where—
(a) an antisocial behaviour order is made or varied; or
(b) an interim order is made.
(2) The clerk of the court by which the order is made or varied shall cause a copy of the order as so made or varied to be—
(a) served on the person subject to the order; and
(b) given to the relevant authority on whose application the order was made.

(3) Subsection (4) applies where—
(a) an antisocial behaviour order is revoked; or
(b) an interim order is recalled.

(4) The clerk of the court by which the order is revoked or recalled shall notify—
(a) the person subject to the order; and
(b) the relevant authority on whose application the order was made,
of the revocation or recall.

(5) For the purposes of subsection (2)(a), a copy is served if—
(a) given to the person subject to the order; or
(b) sent to that person by registered post or the recorded delivery service.

(6) For the purposes of subsection (4)(a), the person subject to the order is notified if notification is sent to the person by registered post or the recorded delivery service.

(7) A certificate of posting of a letter sent under subsection (5)(b) or (6) issued by the postal operator concerned shall be sufficient evidence of the sending of the letter on the day specified in such certificate.

(8) In subsection (7), "postal operator" has the meaning given by section 125(1) of the Postal Services Act 2000 (c.26).

DEFINITIONS
"antisocial behaviour order":   s.4(4)

GENERAL NOTE
This section imposes an obligation on the relevant clerk of court to notify both the local authority or registered social landlord who applied for an ASBO or any other order relating to it and the person affected by the order about the making, variation, recall or revocation of an order or, as appropriate, an interim order. Although this section requires limited notification the *Guidance on Antisocial Behaviour Orders* suggests a wider range of notification by the local authority or registered social landlord (paras 120–122). That there are extensive powers to publicise the granting of orders is confirmed by *R. (on the application of Stanley) v Commissioner of Police of the Metropolis* [2004] EWHC 2229. Although in this case the point was made that the publicity must pursue a legitimate aim and be proportionate, publicity across a whole borough was regarded as being justified, even though this went considerably beyond the area actually affected by the antisocial behaviour. Legitimate objectives pursued by publicity included reassurance of the public that action was being taken, assistance in enforcement by identifying those subject to orders and deterrence (see paras 40–43). It should be noted that the views of the High Court do not appear to be shared by the Council of Europe Commissioner for Human Rights who suggests that "It seems to me, however, to be entirely disproportionate to aggressively inform members of the community who have no knowledge of the offending behaviour, and who are not affected by it, of the application of ASBOs." (*Report on a Visit to the United Kingdom*, March 2005, http://www.coe.int/T/E/Commissioner_H.R/Communication_Unit/CommDH%282005%296_E.doc)

Breach of orders

Breach of orders
    9.—(1) Subject to subsection (3), a person who—
(a) is subject to an antisocial behaviour order or an interim order; and
(b) without reasonable excuse, does anything that the order to which the person is subject prohibits the person from doing, shall be guilty of an offence.

(2) A person guilty of an offence under subsection (1) shall be liable—
(a) on summary conviction, to imprisonment for a term not exceeding 6 months or to a fine not exceeding the statutory maximum or to both; or

(b) on conviction on indictment, to imprisonment for a term not exceeding 5 years or to a fine or to both.

(3) If—

(a) otherwise than under subsection (1), the thing done by the person constitutes an offence (a "separate offence"); and

(b) the person is charged with the separate offence,
    the person shall not be liable to be proceeded against for an offence under subsection (1).

(4) Subject to subsection (5), if a person is convicted of a separate offence, the court which sentences the person for that offence shall, in determining the appropriate sentence or disposal, have regard to—

(a) the fact that the separate offence was committed while the person was subject to the antisocial behaviour order or, as the case may be, interim order;

(b) the number of antisocial behaviour orders and interim orders to which the person was subject at the time of commission of the separate offence;

(c) any previous conviction of the person for an offence under subsection (1); and

(d) the extent to which the sentence or disposal in respect of any previous conviction of the person differed, by virtue of this subsection, from that which the court would have imposed but for this section.

(5) The court shall not, under subsection (4)(a), have regard to the fact that the separate offence was committed while the person was subject to the antisocial behaviour order or, as the case may be, the interim order unless that fact is libelled in the indictment or, as the case may be, specified in the complaint.

(6) The fact that the separate offence was committed while the person was subject to an antisocial behaviour order or, as the case may be, an interim order, shall, unless challenged—

(a) in the case of proceedings on indictment, by the giving of notice of a preliminary objection in accordance with section 71(2) or 72(6)(b)(i) of the Criminal Procedure (Scotland) Act 1995 (c.46); or

(b) in summary proceedings, by preliminary objection before the person's plea is recorded,
    be held as admitted.

DEFINITIONS
"antisocial behaviour order":   s.4(4)
"separate offence":   subs.(3)(a)

GENERAL NOTE
Breach of an ASBO or an interim ASBO is in itself an offence punishable as set out in subs.(2) although this need not involve activity which is itself criminal. It will be a defence to any prosecution for breach that there was a reasonable excuse, this might be related to illness or disability (subs.(1)(b)). The behaviour constituting the breach may amount to a separate offence and where a person is charged with this offence they cannot also be prosecuted for the simple breach of the order, but rather, as indicated in subs.(3) the fact that the offence was committed whilst subject to the order will be an aggravating factor in considering the sentence to be imposed for the offence. Additional aggravating factors include the number of ASBOs to which the person was subject and any previous convictions for breach of an ASBO. The existence of the order can, however, only be considered by the court if it is either specified in a complaint or libelled in an indictment.

Breach of orders: prohibition on detention of children
    10.—(1) The Criminal Procedure (Scotland) Act 1995 (c.46) shall be amended as follows.

(2) In subsection (2) of section 44 (detention of children), after "offence" there shall be inserted "(other than, if the child is under the age of 16 years, an offence under section 9(1) of the Antisocial Behaviour etc. (Scotland) Act 2004 (asp 8) or that section as applied by section 234AA(11) of this Act)".

(3) In section 208 (detention of children convicted on indictment), after "Act" there shall be inserted "and subsection (3) below".

(4) At the end of section 208 there shall be added—

"(3) If the child is under the age of 16 years, the power conferred by subsection (1) above shall not be exercisable in respect of a conviction for an offence under section 9(1) of the Antisocial Behaviour etc. (Scotland) Act 2004 (asp 8) or that section as applied by section 234AA(11) of this Act.".

GENERAL NOTE
Notwithstanding the effect of s.9(2) providing for imprisonment on breach of an ASBO, children under 16 cannot be detained on conviction of such a breach. The amendments included here achieve that in respect of the sheriff summary court (disapplying s.44 of the Criminal Procedure (Scotland) Act 1995 (c.46)) and solemn courts (disapplying s.208 of the Criminal Procedure (Scotland) Act 1995).

Breach of orders: arrest without warrant
11.—(1) Where a constable reasonably believes that a person is committing or has committed an offence under section 9(1), the constable may arrest the person without warrant.

(2) Subsection (1) is without prejudice to any power of arrest conferred by law apart from that subsection.

GENERAL NOTE
This section simply confers a power of arrest without warrant in cases of breach of an ASBO or interim ASBO.

Orders in respect of children

Sheriff's power to refer case to children's hearing
12.—(1) Where the sheriff makes an antisocial behaviour order or an interim order in respect of a child, the sheriff may require the Principal Reporter to refer the child's case to a children's hearing.

(2) The Children (Scotland) Act 1995 (c.36) shall be amended in accordance with subsections (3) to (5).

(3) After paragraph (l) of section 52(2) (children requiring compulsory measures of supervision) there shall be inserted—

"(m) is a child to whom subsection (2A) below applies.
(2A) This subsection applies to a child where—
(a) a requirement is made of the Principal Reporter under section 12(1) of the Antisocial Behaviour etc. (Scotland) Act 2004 (asp 8) (power of sheriff to require Principal Reporter to refer case to children's hearing) in respect of the child's case; and
(b) the child is not subject to a supervision requirement.".

(4) After section 65(1) (referral of case to children's hearing), there shall be inserted—
"(1A) Where the Principal Reporter is satisfied that the ground specified in section 52(2)(m) of this Act is established in respect

of any child, he shall be taken to be satisfied as to the matter mentioned in section 65(1)(a) in respect of the child.".

(5) In section 73(8) (arrangements to review supervision requirement)—
(a) in paragraph (a)(v), after "months;" there shall be inserted—
"(aa) where—
    (i) a requirement is made of the Principal Reporter under section 12(1) of the Antisocial Behaviour etc. (Scotland) Act 2004 (asp 8) (power of sheriff to require Principal Reporter to refer case to children's hearing) in respect of the child's case; and
    (ii) the child is subject to a supervision requirement,
arrange for a children's hearing to review the supervision requirement;";
(b) in paragraph (b), for "that" there shall be substituted "any such".

DEFINITIONS
"antisocial behaviour order":   s.4(4)

GENERAL NOTE
    Where an order is made in respect of someone under 16 the sheriff has the power to require that a children's hearing be held to consider the case of the child. This may either be a hearing to consider the case of a child currently not subject to a supervision requirement (the effect of subss (3) and (4), the latter has the effect that a child referred in this way is deemed to be in need of compulsory measures of supervision and therefore requires the reporter to arrange a hearing) or a review hearing where the child is already subject to a supervision requirement (the effect of subs.(5)). Once the case is referred to a hearing it will then be up to the hearing to decide whether to either impose a supervision requirement or to change an existing requirement. The making of an ASBO will not in itself be a ground for referral to a children's hearing (though the behaviour underlying it probably will be) nor will it automatically trigger a review of an existing supervision requirement.

Sheriff's power to make parenting order

13.—(1) Where a sheriff makes an antisocial behaviour order in respect of a child, the sheriff may, where subsection (2) applies, make a parenting order in respect of a parent of the child.

(2) This subsection applies where—
(a) the sheriff is satisfied that the making of the order is desirable in the interests of preventing the child from engaging in further antisocial behaviour; and
(b) the Scottish Ministers have notified the court that the local authority for the area in which the parent ordinarily resides has made arrangements that would enable the order to be complied with.

(3) In this section—
"parent" has the meaning given by section 117; and
"parenting order" has the meaning given by section 103(1).

DEFINITIONS
"antisocial behaviour order":   s.4(4)
"parent":   s.117
"parenting order":   s.103(1)

GENERAL NOTE
    The sheriff is empowered to make a parenting order (see General Note to s.103) at the same time as an ASBO is made in respect of a child. The preconditions for the order are set out in subs.(2), and it is to be noted that this power will only be exercisable where the local authority has arrangements in place to provide the support and services required under a parenting order.

Provision of information and records

Provision of information to local authorities
 14.—(1) Where by virtue of subsection (2)(b) of section 8 a registered social landlord—
 (a) is given a copy of an antisocial behaviour order as made or varied; or
 (b) is given a copy of an interim order,
 it shall give a copy to each relevant local authority.
 (2) Where by virtue of subsection (4)(b) of that section a registered social landlord—
 (a) is notified of the revocation of an antisocial behaviour order; or
 (b) is notified of the recall of an interim order,
 it shall notify each relevant local authority of the date on which the order was revoked or recalled.
 (3) In this section "relevant local authority" means a local authority whose area includes the premises referred to in section 4(13)(b) in relation to any person for whose protection the order was made.

DEFINITIONS
"antisocial behaviour order":   s.4(4)
"relevant local authority":   subs.(3)

GENERAL NOTE
 This section requires registered social landlords to pass on to the local authority any notifications it receives under s.8 of the making, variation, revocation or recall of an ASBO. This not only provides information to the authority which may be relevant for its own records, but also enables them to keep the register of ASBOs required by s.15.

Records of orders
 15.—(1) A local authority shall keep records of—
 (a) each antisocial behaviour order; and
 (b) each interim order,
 of which the authority is given a copy by virtue of section 8(2)(b) or 14(1).
 (2) A record kept under subsection (1) shall specify—
 (a) the person in respect of whom the order was made;
 (b) the prohibitions imposed by the order;
 (c) if the record relates to an antisocial behaviour order—
  (i) whether a prohibition is indefinite or for a definite period and where it is for a period, that period;
  (ii) where the authority is, by virtue of section 8(2)(b) or, as the case may be, 14(1), given a copy of the order as varied, the variation and its date; and
  (iii) where the authority is, by virtue of section 8(4)(b) or, as the case may be, 14(2), notified of the revocation of the order, the date on which it was revoked;
 (d) if the record relates to an interim order, where the authority is, by virtue of section 8(4)(b) or, as the case may be, 14(2), notified of the recall of the order, the date on which it was recalled; and
 (e) such other matters relating to the order as the Scottish Ministers may prescribe in regulations.
 (3) A local authority shall, on a request to do so being made to it by a person mentioned in subsection (4), disclose to that person information contained in a record kept under subsection (1).
 (4) Those persons are—

(a) the Scottish Ministers;
(b) the Principal Reporter;
(c) any other local authority;
(d) a chief constable; and
(e) a registered social landlord.

GENERAL NOTE
A record of orders, containing the information specified in subs.(2), must be kept by local authorities. Requests for disclosure of records can be made by any of those listed in subs.(4). This is without prejudice to the notification requirements imposed on authorities under the *Guidance on Antisocial Behaviour Orders* (see General Note to s.8).

Guidance and research

Guidance in relation to antisocial behaviour orders
16. A person (other than a court) shall, in discharging functions by virtue of this Part (other than section 13), have regard to any guidance given by the Scottish Ministers about—
(a) the discharge of those functions; and
(b) matters arising in connection with the discharge of those functions.

GENERAL NOTE
This guidance is in the form of *Guidance on Antisocial Behaviour Orders*, which can be found at: http://www.scotland.gov.uk/library5/social/asbsg.pdf.

Arrangement of study into operation of Part
17.—(1) The Scottish Ministers shall—
(a) arrange for the carrying out of a study into the operation of this Part; and
(b) lay a report on the results of the study before the Scottish Parliament within 3 years of the date on which the whole of the Part was first in force.
(2) The Scottish Ministers shall make such preparations for the carrying out of the study as are necessary to enable the study to commence as soon as the whole of the Part is in force; and such preparations may include, in particular, the instruction of a research team and the formation of a research advisory group to assist in the direction of the study.

GENERAL NOTE
This section, together with another section requiring research into the operation of Pt 3 of the Act, were added at Stage 3 of the Act's progress through the Scottish Parliament. Some research already exists, at least into the frequency of use of ASBOs by different local authorities which shows considerable differences in the use of ASBOs (Chartered Institute of Housing, *Targetting Anti-Social Behaviour*, October 2003, confirmed by later figures see Scottish Parliament, Written Answers, October 28, 2004). These differences prompted the Minister (Margaret Curran) to remark that she was "keen to know why some local authorities perform extraordinarily well in tackling antisocial behaviour through the use of ASBOs, but others do not" (Official Report, June 17, 2004, col.9203). This comment perhaps casts doubts as to the effect of any research as the report referred to concluded that:
"The use of ASBOs varies across Scotland. This does not mean, however, that local authorities not using ASBOs are not tackling anti-social behaviour effectively. They may be employing alternative methods to deal with the issues. ASBOs are only one tool in the armoury of actions available to address anti-social behaviour." (p.22).
Subsequent research confirms the wide variation in practice in use of ASBOs (*Use of Antisocial Behaviour Orders in Scotland*, DTZ Pieda Consulting and Heriot Watt University, March 2005,). This is available at: http://www.scotland.gov.uk/Resource/Doc/1101/0010249.pdf

Interpretation

Interpretation of Part 2

18. In this Part—

"affected person" has the meaning given by section 4(7);

"antisocial behaviour order" has the meaning given by section 4(5);

"child" means a person who is under the age of 16 years;

"interim order" has the meaning given by section 7(2)(c);

"relevant authority" means—

(a) a local authority; or

(b) a registered social landlord;

"relevant consultees" means—

(a) in relation to an antisocial behaviour order sought or made on the application of a local authority—

    (i) the chief constable of the police force for the area which includes the area of the authority;

    (ii) the chief constable of each police force for an area where there is an affected person;

    (iii) each local authority in whose area there is an affected person; and

    (iv) if the person in respect of whom the order is sought or made is a child, the Principal Reporter;

(b) in relation to an antisocial behaviour order sought or made on the application of a registered social landlord—

    (i) the chief constable of the police force for the area in which the person in respect of whom the order is sought or made resides or appears to reside; and

    (ii) if that person is a child, the Principal Reporter;

"specified person" has the meaning given by section 4(1).

PART 3

DISPERSAL OF GROUPS

GENERAL NOTE

This part of the Act was probably the most controversial, starting from the initial consultations on the proposed legislation. There was opposition not only from charities involved in working with children, but also from the police at all levels (see, for example, the evidence given to the Justice 2 Committee at Stage 1, Official Report, January 6, 2004, cols 424–430, 434–440). This opposition culminated in an unsuccessful attempt to remove the whole of this part of the Act at Stage 3. Most of the opposition was linked to the claim that adequate powers already existed under pre-existing law, particularly, for example, under the law relating to breach of the peace. In this context it interesting to note the comment made by the Minister (Margaret Curran) that 'the provisions of part 3 neither provide sweeping new powers *nor do they add anything to existing powers* (Official Report, June 17, 2004, col.9208, emphasis added).

The *Guidance* issued on this part of the Act notes that the use of these powers will have to be considered carefully to avoid simply displacing the problem and that they are not intended to be used in isolation, but rather as a package of measures to tackle antisocial behaviour.

For a discussion of the human rights implications of this type of provision and concerns about their compatibility with the European Convention on Human Rights see House of Commons/House of Lords Joint Committee on Human Rights, 13th Report 2002–2003, *The Anti-social Behaviour Bill*, 2002–2003 HC 120, paras 29–35. It should be born in mind that even if the general provisions are compatible with the European Convention it may still be the case that using the powers in an individual case infringes rights in a way which is not justified by a pressing social need. In such a case there would be an infringement of Convention rights for which aggrieved parties would have a remedy.

At the time of writing (June 2005) these powers have only been used in one area.

Authorisations and powers

Authorisations

19.—(1) Subsection (2) applies where a police officer of or above the rank of superintendent (a "senior police officer") has reasonable grounds for believing—

(a) that any members of the public have been alarmed or distressed as a result of the presence or behaviour of groups of two or more persons in public places in any locality in the officer's police area (the "relevant locality"); and

(b) that antisocial behaviour is a significant, persistent and serious problem in the relevant locality.

(2) The senior police officer may authorise the exercise of the powers conferred by section 21—

(a) during a specified period;

(b) on specified days that fall within a specified period;

(c) between specified times that fall within a specified period.

(3) An authorisation under subsection (2)—

(a) shall be in writing;

(b) shall be signed by the senior police officer giving it; and

(c) shall specify—

    (i) the relevant locality;

    (ii) the grounds on which the authorisation is given; and

    (iii) when the powers are exercisable.

(4) Before giving an authorisation under subsection (2) the senior police officer who proposes to give it shall ensure that any local authority whose area includes the whole or part of the relevant locality is consulted.

(5) A period specified under subsection (2) shall not exceed 3 months.

(6) In subsection (2), "specified" means specified by the senior police officer.

DEFINITIONS

"public place":	s.25(1)
"relevant locality":	subs.(1)(a)
"senior police officer":	subs.(1)

GENERAL NOTE

This section permits a police officer of the rank of superintendent or above to designate a particular area (the relevant locality) within which the police will be able to exercise their right of dispersal under s.21. Before making such an authorisation the officer must:

(a) consult the local authority (subs.(4)), though consultation with other community groups is not ruled out. (*Guidance on Dispersal of Groups*, paras 31–33)

(b) be satisfied as to the matters set out in subs.(1)(a). In this context the wide definition of 'public place' in s.25(1) should be noted. It includes private premises to which the public have access, whether on payment or not, as well as the common parts of tenement buildings, roads and doorways. In addition, it covers premises to which individuals have obtained unlawful access.

(c) be satisfied that the requirements of subs.(1)(b) are met. The requirement that antisocial behaviour be serious was added at stage 3, and it is perhaps difficult to imagine conduct which is significant (defined in the *Guidance* as 'of considerable effect or importance' (para.15)) and persistent (see *Guidance*, para.20, suggesting a guideline that it has occurred on six days out of 21), but not also serious.

The authorisation must specify its duration (not more than three months), the grounds for making it and the area covered. In determining this latter element the *Guidance* notes that one consideration will be the practicability of dispersal in or from the area selected (para.38). In addition, the authorisation must specify the periods during which it is effective and when the police will be able to rely on it to disperse groups. Thus, for example, the authorisation might be restricted to Fridays, Saturdays and Sundays, or to a specific period each day.

Authorisations: supplementary

20.—(1) Before the powers conferred by section 21 become exercisable by virtue of an authorisation, the senior police officer who gave the authorisation shall ensure that an authorisation notice is—

(a) published in a newspaper circulating in the relevant locality; and

(b) displayed in some conspicuous place or places within the relevant locality.

(2) An "authorisation notice" is a notice which—

(a) states that authorisation has been given;

(b) specifies the relevant locality; and

(c) specifies when the powers may be exercised.

(3) An authorisation may be withdrawn by—

(a) the senior police officer who gave it; or

(b) any police officer whose police area includes the relevant locality and whose rank is the same as or higher than that of the senior police officer mentioned in paragraph (a).

(4) Before withdrawing, under subsection (3), an authorisation, the police officer who proposes to withdraw the authorisation shall ensure that any local authority whose area includes the whole or part of the relevant locality is consulted.

(5) The withdrawal of an authorisation shall not affect the exercise, by virtue of the authorisation, of any power which occurred before the withdrawal.

(6) The giving or withdrawal of an authorisation shall not prevent the giving of a further authorisation in respect of a locality which includes the whole or any part of the relevant locality to which the earlier authorisation relates.

(7) In this section, "authorisation" means an authorisation under section 19.

DEFINITIONS
"authorisation notice":   subs.(2)

GENERAL NOTE
Before the police can use the powers of dispersal in s.21 in an authorised area the authorisation must be publicized in the manner set out in subs.(1). This section also provides for the authorisation to be withdrawn by the officer who issued it or by an officer of the same or a higher rank after consultation with the local authority (subss (3) and (4)). Withdrawal might be appropriate if there had been a significant reduction in antisocial behaviour in the locality.

Powers exercisable in pursuance of authorisations

21.—(1) Where a constable has reasonable grounds for believing that the presence or behaviour of a group of two or more persons in any public place in the relevant locality is causing or is likely to cause alarm or distress to any members of the public, the constable may exercise a power mentioned in subsection (3).

(2) In determining whether to exercise a power mentioned in subsection (3) a constable shall have regard to whether the exercise of the power would be likely to result in the persons in the group causing less alarm and distress to members of the public in the relevant locality than if the power were not exercised.

(3) Subject to subsection (5), the constable may give—

(a) a direction requiring the persons in the group to disperse;

(b) a direction requiring any of those persons whose place of residence is not within the relevant locality to leave the relevant locality or any part of the relevant locality;

(c) a direction prohibiting any of those persons whose place of residence is not within the relevant locality from returning to the relevant locality or any part of the relevant locality during such period (not exceeding 24 hours) from the giving of the direction as the constable may specify.

(4) The constable may require a direction under paragraph (a) or (b) of subsection (3) to be complied with—

(a) immediately or by such time as the constable may specify;

(b) in such way as may be so specified.

(5) A direction under subsection (3) may not be given in respect of a group of persons—

(a) who are engaged in conduct which is lawful under section 220 of the Trade Union and Labour Relations (Consolidation) Act 1992 (c.52); or

(b) who are taking part in a procession in respect of which—

(i) written notice has been given in accordance with subsections (2) and (3) of section 62 of the Civic Government (Scotland) Act 1982 (c.45);

(ii) by virtue of subsection (6) or (7) of that section such notice is not required to be given.

DEFINITIONS

"group":subs:	(1)
"relevant locality":	s.19(1)(a)

GENERAL NOTE

This section sets out the circumstances in which the power to disperse a group authorised by an order made under s.19 can be exercised. Although much of the discussion prior to and during passage of the Act focused on the problem of relatively large groups of young people causing problems, for the exercise of this power a group can be as little as two people. The section does not actually require them to be behaving in a way that is antisocial, it can be enough that the presence of a group is likely to cause alarm or distress, perhaps based on past experience of the behaviour of the group. Indeed, applying s.25(2), it can be seen that all that is required is that the presence or behaviour of *one* person in a group has this effect before the power can be exercised. This has to be balanced by an assessment of whether dispersal will have the effect of reducing the alarm and distress to people in the relevant locality (subs.(2)). It should be noted that the possibility of recongregation and antisocial behaviour outwith this area is not a consideration, unless it will affect people within the relevant locality (see *Guidance on Dispersal of Groups*, paras 51–52).

Subsections (3) and (4) set out the content of the dispersal power, this includes not only requiring a group to disperse, but also requiring individuals to leave the locality (subs.(3)(b)) and to prohibit return within a period of up to 24 hours (subs.(3)(c)). Subsection (4) allows the police to control the dispersal, so as, for example, to minimise any distress or alarm caused to members of the public. That the instructions can be given orally and also withdrawn is clarified by s.22, which also provides that failure to comply with an instruction is itself an offence.

Subsection (5) sets out exceptions to the power, including industrial disputes and certain processions, including, for example Orange Walks, though these are the subject of other controlling legislation and common law provisions dealing with disorder.

Finally, the power to disperse must be exercised within the boundaries set out by the equal opportunities requirement of s.140.

Powers under section 21: supplementary

22.—(1) A direction under section 21—

(a) may be given orally;

(b) may be given to any person individually or to two or more persons together; and

(c) may be withdrawn or varied by the constable who gave it.

(2) A person who, without reasonable excuse, knowingly contravenes a direction given to the person under section 21 shall be guilty of an offence and liable on summary conviction to—

(a) a fine not exceeding level 4 on the standard scale; or

(b) imprisonment for a term not exceeding 3 months,

or to both.

(3) Where a constable reasonably suspects that a person has committed or is committing an offence under subsection (2), the constable may arrest the person without warrant.

(4) Subsection (3) is without prejudice to any power of arrest conferred by law apart from that subsection.

GENERAL NOTE

This section clarifies the way in which instructions to disperse may be given and provides for failure to comply with an instruction to be an offence. Further guidance is provided in the *Guidance on Dispersal of Groups* (paras 49–62), which indicates for example that the police should also notify a group of the existence of the s.19 authorisation and the boundaries of the relevant locality. It also suggests that a leaflet explaining the power might be handed out to overcome problems arising from claims that the instruction to disperse was misunderstood (para.58).

Guidance and research

Guidance in relation to dispersal of groups

23.—(1) A person exercising a power by virtue of this Part shall, in the exercise of the power, have regard to any guidance given by the Scottish Ministers about—

(a) the exercise of the power; and

(b) any other matter relating to the power.

(2) The Scottish Ministers shall lay before the Scottish Parliament a copy of any guidance such as is mentioned in subsection (1).

GENERAL NOTE

The guidance issued shortly before implementation of this part of the Act is the *Guidance on Dispersal of Groups*, which can be found at: http://www.scotland.gov.uk/library5/social/asbd.pdf.

Operation of Part: arrangement of study

24.—(1) The Scottish Ministers shall—

(a) arrange for the carrying out of a study into the operation of this Part; and

(b) lay a report on the results of the study before the Scottish Parliament within 3 years of the date on which the whole of the Part was first in force.

(2) The Scottish Ministers shall make such preparations for the carrying out of the study as are necessary to enable the study to commence as soon as the whole of the Part is in force; and such preparations may include, in particular, the instruction of a research team and the formation of a research advisory group to assist in the direction of the study.

GENERAL NOTE

This section was introduced at Stage 3 of the debate on the Act. It reflects the controversial nature of the provisions of this part of the Act and also considerable scepticism as to their effectiveness (see the debate in Official Report, June 17, 2004, cols 9200–9204).

Interpretation

Interpretation of Part 3
25.—(1) In this Part—

"public place" means any place to which the public have access at the material time (whether on payment of a fee or otherwise); and includes—
  (a) the doorways or entrances of premises abutting on any such place;
  (b) a road (as defined in section 151(1) of the Roads (Scotland) Act 1984 (c.54));
  (c) any common passage, close, court, stair or yard pertinent to any tenement or group of separately owned houses; and
  (d) any place to which the public do not have access but to which persons have unlawfully gained access; and
"relevant locality" has the meaning given by section 19(1)(a).

(2) In this Part, any reference to the presence or behaviour of a group of persons includes a reference to the presence or behaviour of any one or more of the persons in the group.

PART 4

CLOSURE OF PREMISES

GENERAL NOTE
  This part allows for the closure of premises, broadly defined to include open spaces but not including roads or footpaths, even where these are disused. Closure is initially effected by a closure notice served by a police officer of the rank of superintendent or above. This is then followed up by application to the sheriff for a closure order. The effect of a notice or order is, subject to limited exceptions, to prohibit access to the closed premises. The object of these powers is to allow the closure of premises which are associated with antisocial behaviour. Examples might include public houses associated with disorder or excessive noise or disturbance to surrounding residents (an attempt to exclude licensed premises from the ambit of this part of the Act was rejected at stage 3), or a flat used as a brothel or as a base for dealing in or consumption of drugs.
  It is interesting to contrast the ease with which a person can be removed from their accommodation under this part of the Act with the extensive procedural protection offered to tenants under the Housing (Scotland) Act 1988 and the Housing (Scotland) Act 2001. In the case of residential properties there will be the possibility of infringement of rights under Art.8 of the European Convention on Human Rights if care is not exercised in respect of the evidential basis for closure and proper consideration is not given to those affected by the closure. On the need to proceed with caution see *Moat Housing Group Ltd v Harris & Anr* [2005] EWCA Civ 287.

Closure notices

Authorisation of closure notice
  26.—(1) Subject to subsections (2) and (3), a senior police officer may authorise the service of a notice (a "closure notice") prohibiting access to premises by any person other than—
  (a) a person who habitually resides in the premises; or
  (b) the owner of the premises.
  (2) The Scottish Ministers may by regulations specify premises or descriptions of premises in respect of which an authorisation under subsection (1) may not be given.
  (3) A senior police officer may authorise the service of a closure notice only where the senior police officer—

(a) has reasonable grounds for believing that—
    (i) at any time during the immediately preceding 3 months a person has engaged in antisocial behaviour on the premises; and
    (ii) the use of the premises is associated with the occurrence of relevant harm; and
(b) is satisfied that—
    (i) the local authority for the area in which the premises are situated has been consulted; and
    (ii) reasonable steps have been taken to establish the identity of any person who lives on, has control of, has responsibility for or has an interest in the premises.

(4) An authorisation given under subsection (1) shall, if given orally, be confirmed by the senior police officer in writing as soon as is practicable.

DEFINITIONS

"antisocial behaviour":	s.143
"premises":	s.40
"relevant harm":	s.40
"senior police officer":	s.19(1)

GENERAL NOTE

Before a closure notice can be served, it must be authorised by an officer of the rank of superintendent or above. The order can only be authorised if the officer:

(i) Has reasonable grounds to believe that someone has engaged in antisocial behaviour on the premises. It seems clear from this requirement that the antisocial behaviour must take place on the premises rather than in their vicinity or being associated with them. For example, regular disorder outside licensed premises could not be used as a basis for a closure order unless there was also some antisocial behaviour on the premises. AND

(ii) Has reasonable grounds to believe that the use of the premises is associated either with significant and persistent disorder or with significant, persistent and serious nuisance to members of the public.

Both of these requirements have to be fulfilled so that while the public house example in (i) above might fulfil the second requirement that in itself could not be the basis of a closure notice. Examples of relevant harm are considered in paras 8–10 of the *Guidance on Closure of Premises* (though it is not entirely clear from the examples given that the need to meet both requirements is fully appreciated).

In addition, the officer will need to be satisfied that the local authority has been consulted and that reasonable steps have been taken to identify any of the people listed in subs.(3)(b)(ii), and will have to have considered the checklist set out in Annex A of the *Guidance on Closure of Premises*. Consultation with the local authority will have to cover matters such as the alternative accommodation needs of anyone residing in the premises and measures to resolve the problem in the longer term.

The effect of the notice is to prohibit access to the premises except by the owner or by someone resident there.

Service etc.

27.—(1) This section applies where the service of a closure notice in respect of premises is authorised under section 26(1).

(2) The closure notice shall be served by a constable who shall do so by—
(a) fixing a copy of the notice to—
    (i) at least one prominent place on the premises;
    (ii) each normal means of access to the premises; and
    (iii) any outbuildings that appear to the constable to be used with or as part of the premises; and
(b) giving a copy of the notice to—

    (i) each person identified in pursuance of section 26(3)(b)(ii); and

    (ii) every other person appearing to the constable to be a person of a description mentioned in that subsection.

(3) If after having made reasonable enquiries at the time of serving the closure notice under subsection (2) the constable believes that the access of any person who occupies—

(a) any other part of the building; or

(b) any other structure,

    in which the premises are situated would be impeded by the making of an order under section 30, the constable shall give a copy of the notice to that person.

(4) Failure to comply with subsection (2)(b) or (3) shall not affect the validity of the closure notice.

(5) The closure notice shall—

(a) specify the premises to which it relates;

(b) state that access to the premises by any person other than—

    (i) a person who habitually resides in the premises; or

    (ii) the owner of the premises,

    is prohibited;

(c) state that failure to comply with the notice amounts to an offence;

(d) state that an application is to be made under section 28 for the closure of the premises;

(e) specify such matters about that application as may be prescribed in rules of court;

(f) explain the effects of an order made under section 30; and

(g) give information about the names of, and means of contacting, persons who and organisations which provide advice about housing and legal matters in the locality of the premises.

DEFINITIONS
"closure notice":   s.26(1)
"premises":   s.40

GENERAL NOTE
  This sets out the content of and requirements for service of a closure notice. In terms of the latter the only absolute requirement for the notice to be effective is that it is affixed to the premises in accordance with subs.(2)(a). No duration is specified for the effectiveness of a closure notice, though by implication it will lapse if an application for a closure order is not made on the first court day after the affixation of copy notices (s.28(3)). Where such an application is made the notice will remain in force until it is determined. Additional requirements for the content of a closure notice are set out in Rule 3.27.6 of the Act of Sederunt (Summary Applications, Statutory Applications and Appeals etc. Rules)1999 (SI 1999/929) inserted by (Act of Sederunt (Summary Applications, Statutory Applications and Appeals etc Rules) Amendment (Antisocial Behaviour (Scotland) Act 2004), 2004 (SSI 2004/455).

  One of these additional requirements is that the notice specifies the date and time of the court hearing under s.28. As pointed out in *McIlravie v Wallace*, 2005 S.L.T. (Sh Ct) 2, this requires specification of a hearing which has not yet been fixed and which may not take place.

Closure orders

Application to sheriff

  28.—(1) Subsection (2) applies where paragraph (a) of section 27(2) is fulfilled in relation to a closure notice.

  (2) A senior police officer shall apply to the sheriff for a closure order in respect of the premises specified in the notice.

(3) Subject to subsection (4), an application under subsection (2) shall be made no later than the first court day after the day on which paragraph (a) of section 27(2) is fulfilled in relation to the notice.

(4) The sheriff may, on cause shown, allow an application which is late to proceed.

(5) An application under subsection (2) shall—

(a) specify the premises in respect of which the closure order is sought;

(b) state the grounds on which the application is made; and

(c) be accompanied by such supporting evidence (whether in documentary form or otherwise) as will enable the sheriff to determine the application.

DEFINITIONS

"closure order":   s.29

"court day":   s.40

GENERAL NOTE

Once a closure notice has been served an officer of the rank of superintendent or above can apply to the sheriff for a closure order. This application must normally be made no later than the first court day after service of the notice, though the sheriff may allow a later application (subs.(4)). The effect and duration of a closure order are set out in s.29.

Closure orders

29.—(1) A closure order is an order that the premises specified in the order are closed to all persons for such period not exceeding 3 months as is specified in the order.

(2) A closure order may be made only in respect of all or any part of premises that are the subject of a closure notice.

(3) A closure order may include such provision as the sheriff (or, on appeal, the sheriff principal) making it considers appropriate about access to any part of the building or structure of which the premises specified in the order form part.

GENERAL NOTE

A closure order closes the premises completely for an initial period of up to three months, though this can subsequently be extended subject to a maximum duration of six months (s.32). In addition to the closure order the sheriff also has the power to regulate access to other parts of the building in which the closed premises are situated.

Application: determination

30.—(1) On an application under section 28, the sheriff may, if satisfied that the conditions mentioned in subsection (2) are met, make a closure order in respect of premises.

(2) Those conditions are—

(a) that a person has engaged in antisocial behaviour on the premises;

(b) that the use of the premises is associated with the occurrence of relevant harm; and

(c) that the making of the order is necessary to prevent the occurrence of such relevant harm for the period specified in the order.

(3) The sheriff shall, in determining whether to make a closure order in respect of premises, have regard to—

(a) the ability of any person who habitually resides in the premises to find alternative accommodation; and

(b) any vulnerability of any person such as is mentioned in paragraph (a) who has not been engaged in antisocial behaviour which has occurred in the premises.

(4) Subject to subsection (5), the sheriff shall determine an application under section 28 no later than the second court day after the day on which the application is made.

(5) The sheriff may postpone determination of the application for a period of not more than 14 days to enable a person mentioned in subsection (6) to show why a closure order should not be made.

(6) Those persons are—

(a) the occupier of the premises specified in the closure notice upon which the application proceeds;

(b) any person who has control of or responsibility for those premises;

(c) any other person with an interest in those premises.

(7) Where, under subsection (5), the sheriff postpones determination of an application, the sheriff may order that the closure notice upon which the application proceeds shall continue in effect until the determination of the application.

DEFINITIONS

| "premises": | s.40 |
| "relevant harm": | s.40 |

GENERAL NOTE

Normally an application for a closure order must be determined no later than the second court day after the application is made, but the sheriff has the power to continue the application for up to 14 days to allow representations from the occupier of the premises, anyone with control or responsibility for the premises or anyone else with an interest in them, for example, the owner.

Three preconditions must be met before an order can be made:

(a) that a person has behaved in an antisocial manner on the premises;

(b) that use of the premises is associated with either with significant and persistent disorder or with significant, persistent and serious nuisance to members of the public.

(c) making the order is necessary to prevent this.

Even if these conditions are fulfilled the sheriff has discretion to decide whether to make an order. In exercising this discretion he/she has to consider the ability of anyone living in the premises to find alternative accommodation and any vulnerability of a resident who has not been involved in the antisocial behaviour. For example, if the closure order is sought in relation to a flat used for drugs dealing, there will be issues about the effect of this on a partner of the person involved in drug dealing who has not themselves been so involved and who would be rendered homeless by the closure order.

It has been held that making a closure order engages Articles 6 and 8 of the European Convention on Human Rights, as well as Article 1 of Protocol 1 of the Convention. An order can therefore only be made if the evidence suggests that interference with these convention rights can be justified, *Commissioner of the Metropolitan Police v Hooper* [2005] EWHC 340 (Admin). It was also suggested in that case that the 14 day period for adjournment could not be extended and that, despite this, the overall provision was compliant with Art.6. The issue of whether the provisions of subs.(5) displace the common law powers of adjournment enjoyed by courts was raised, but not decided, in *McIlravie v Wallace*, 2005 S.L.T. (Sh Ct) 2. The time limits overall for dealing with closure orders are very tight and there may well be individual cases where an adjournment of more than 14 days would be required to protect the convention rights of someone occupying the premises to be affected by the order. This is particularly the case as the effect of subs.(5) seems to be to shift the burden onto the person affected to show why an order should not be made.

The form in which evidence supporting an application should be presented is commented on in *McIlravie v Wallace*, 2005 S.L.T. (Sh Ct) 2.

Enforcement

31.—(1) Subject to subsection (3), a constable or an authorised person may—

(a) do anything necessary to secure closed premises against entry by any person;

(b) carry out essential maintenance or repairs to closed premises; and
(c) enter the premises for the purposes of paragraph (a) or (b).

(2) A constable or an authorised person acting under subsection (1) may use reasonable force.

(3) An authorised person seeking to enter closed premises under paragraph (c) of subsection (1) for the purpose of paragraph (a) of that subsection shall, if requested to do so by or on behalf of the owner, occupier or other person in charge of the premises, produce evidence of identity and authorisation.

(4) In this section, "authorised person" means a person authorised in writing by the chief constable for the area in which the premises are situated.

DEFINITIONS
"authorised person":   subs.(4)
"closed premises":   s.40

GENERAL NOTE
This section allows action to be taken on the initiative of the police to secure closed premises or to carry out any necessary maintenance to them. Expenses incurred in doing this can be recovered under s.35.

Extension

32.—(1) The sheriff may, on the application of a senior police officer and if satisfied that it is necessary to do so to prevent the occurrence of relevant harm, make an order extending the period for which a closure order has effect for a period not exceeding the maximum period.

(2) In subsection (1), the "maximum period" is the period of 6 months less—
(a) the period specified in the order when it was made; and
(b) if the order has previously been extended, the total period for which it was previously extended.

(3) A senior police officer may make an application under this section only if—
(a) it is made while the closure order has effect; and(b) the senior police officer—
  (i) has reasonable grounds for believing that it is necessary to extend the period for which the closure order has effect for the purpose of preventing the occurrence of relevant harm; and
  (ii) is satisfied that the appropriate local authority has been consulted about the intention to make the application.

DEFINITIONS
"appropriate local authority":   s.40
"closure order":   s.29
"maximum period":   subs.(2)
"relevant harm":   s.40
"senior police officer":   s.19(1)

GENERAL NOTE
A closure order can be extended under this section, subject to an upper limit on duration of six months. The application can only be made if the conditions set out in subs.(3) apply. These require consultation with the local authority and a reasonable belief that the order is still necessary. Once the six month period has elapsed the order cannot be renewed and will lapse. The *Guidance on Closure of Premises* suggests that it is undesirable for closure orders to be

routinely extended beyond the initial maximum three month period (para.83). An application for an extension must be lodged not less than 21 days before the date on which the order is due to expire (Rule 3.27.8 of the Act of Sederunt (Summary Applications, Statutory Applications and Appeals etc. Rules) 1999 (SI 1999/929), added by the Act of Sederunt (Summary Applications, Statutory Applications and Appeals etc Rules) Amendment (Antisocial Behaviour etc. (Scotland) Act 2004), 2004 (SSI 2004/455)).

Revocation

33.—(1) On the application of a person mentioned in subsection (2), the sheriff may if satisfied that a closure order is no longer necessary to prevent the occurrence of relevant harm, revoke the order.

(2) Those persons are—
(a) a senior police officer;
(b) the appropriate local authority;
(c) a person on whom the closure notice relating to the premises in respect of which the closure order has effect was served under section 27(2)(b) or (3); and
(d) a person who has an interest in those premises but on whom the closure notice was not served.

(3) Where an application under this section is made other than by a senior police officer the sheriff shall order service upon such senior police officer as the sheriff considers appropriate.

DEFINITIONS
"appropriate local authority": s.40
"closure notice": s.26(1)
"closure order": s.29
"relevant harm": s.40
"senior police officer": s.19(1)

GENERAL NOTE
A closure order can be revoked by the sheriff if he/she satisfied that it is no longer necessary. The application can be made not only by a senior police officer, but also by the local authority and anyone with an interest in the premises, whether or not they were served with the closure notice which preceded the making of the order.

Access to other premises

34.—(1) The sheriff may, on the application of a person who occupies or owns any part of a building or structure—
(a) in which closed premises are situated; and
(b) in respect of which the closure order does not have effect,
make an order making such provision as the sheriff considers appropriate in relation to access to any part of the building or structure in which the premises in respect of which the closure order has effect are situated.

(2) An application under subsection (1) may be made only while the closure order has effect.

(3) An order under subsection (1) may be made notwithstanding any provision made as mentioned in section 29(3).

DEFINITIONS
"closed premises": s.40
"closure order": s.29

GENERAL NOTE
The effect of a closure order may be to obstruct access through some common part of the building in which the premises are situated, access to the closed premises may be required to

carry out repairs to a common part of the building or the owner of the premises, who may, for example, be the local authority or a registered social landlord, may require access for maintenance or other purposes. In such cases an application can be made to the sheriff to allow access to closed premises. Such an order can be made even where the closure order already contains provision for access.

Reimbursement of expenditure

35.—(1) The sheriff may, on the application of a police authority or a local authority, make such order as the sheriff considers appropriate for the reimbursement by a relevant person of relevant expenditure.

(2) An application under this section may not be made after the expiry of the period of 3 months beginning with the day on which the closure order ceases to have effect.

(3) An application under this section shall be served—
(a) where the application is made—
    (i) by a local authority, on the police authority for the area in which the premises are situated;
    (ii) by a police authority, on the local authority for the area in which the premises are situated; and
(b) on the relevant person.
    (4) In this section—

"relevant person" means the owner of the premises in respect of which the order has (or had) effect; and
"relevant expenditure" means expenditure incurred by the applicant for the purpose of clearing, securing or maintaining the premises in respect of which the closure order has (or had) effect.

DEFINITIONS
"relevant expenditure":   subs.(4)
"relevant person":   subs.(4)

GENERAL NOTE
    Where a local authority or the police (for example under s.31) have incurred expenditure in cleaning, securing or carrying out maintenance on closed premises they can seek an order against the owner to recover this spending.

Appeals

36.—(1) A person who was a party to the proceedings in which the order or decision (as the case may be) was given may appeal against—
(a) a closure order;
(b) an order extending a closure order;
(c) a decision to refuse to make—
    (i) a closure order; or
    (ii) an order extending a closure order;
(d) a decision to revoke a closure order;
(e) a decision to refuse to revoke a closure order;
(f) an order under section 34(1);
(g) a decision to refuse to make an order under section 34(1);
(h) an order under section 35(1); or
(i) a decision to refuse to make an order under section 35(1).
(2) An appeal under this section shall be made to the sheriff principal and shall be made within the period of 21 days beginning with the day on which the order or decision appealed against was made.
(3) On an appeal under this section, the sheriff principal may make any order the sheriff principal considers appropriate.

(4) The decision of the sheriff principal on an appeal under this section shall be final.

(5) In subsection (1), "order extending a closure order" means an order made under section 32(1).

DEFINITIONS
"closure order": s.29
"order extending a closure order": subs.(5)

GENERAL NOTE
Appeal against a decision of the sheriff relating to closure orders or other ancillary orders is to the sheriff principal and no further. The right of appeal is restricted to parties to the proceedings thus excluding someone who falls into one of the categories of person to be notified of a closure notice but to whom notice was not given with the result that they could not become a party to the proceedings.

General

Offences

37.—(1) If without reasonable excuse a person remains on or enters premises—

(a) in contravention of a closure notice; or

(b) in respect of which a closure order has effect,

the person shall be guilty of an offence.

(2) If a person obstructs an authorised person acting in pursuance of section 31(1) the person shall be guilty of an offence.

(3) In subsection (2), "authorised person" has the meaning given by section 31(4).

(4) A person guilty of an offence under subsection (1) or (2) (a "relevant offence") shall be liable on summary conviction—

(a) where the person has not, within the relevant period, been convicted of a previous offence under the same subsection—

(i) to a fine not exceeding level 4 on the standard scale; or

(ii) to imprisonment for a term not exceeding 3 months,

or to both;

(b) where the person has, within the relevant period, been convicted of a previous offence under the same subsection—

(i) to a fine not exceeding the statutory maximum; or

(ii) to imprisonment for a term not exceeding 9 months,

or to both.

(5) In subsection (4), "relevant period" means the period of 2 years ending with the day on which the relevant offence was committed.

DEFINITIONS
"authorised person": s.31(4)
"closure notice": s.26(1)
"closure order": s.29
"relevant period": subs.(5)

GENERAL NOTE
It is an offence to enter or remain in premises where there is a closure notice or order in effect, or to obstruct someone authorised by the police to carry out work related to securing or maintaining such premises. The penalty on conviction is higher if the offender has a prior conviction for an offence under this section within the previous two years (subs.(4)(b)).

Offences under section 37: arrest without warrant

38.—(1) Where a constable reasonably believes that a person is committing or has committed an offence under section 37(1) or (2), the constable may arrest the person without warrant.

(2) Subsection (1) is without prejudice to any power of arrest conferred by law apart from that subsection.

Guidance in relation to closure of premises

39.—A person (other than a court) shall, in discharging functions by virtue of this Part, have regard to any guidance given by the Scottish Ministers about—

(a) the discharge of those functions; or

(b) matters arising in connection with the discharge of those functions.

GENERAL NOTE

The *Guidance on Closure of Premises* can be found at: http://www.scotland.gov.uk/library5/social/asbcp.pdf

Interpretation

Interpretation of Part 4

40. In this Part—

"appropriate local authority" means the local authority for the area in which the premises in respect of which the closure order has effect are situated;

"closure notice" has the meaning given by section 26(1);

"closure order" has the meaning given by section 29(1);

"closed premises" means premises in respect of which a closure order has effect;

"court day" means a day which is not—

(a) a Saturday or Sunday; or

(b) a day which, by virtue of an order made under section 17(1)(b) of the Sheriff Courts (Scotland) Act 1971 (c.58) (as extended by section 8(2) of the Criminal Procedure (Scotland) Act 1995 (c.46)), is a court holiday in respect of criminal business in the sheriff court in question;

"premises" includes—

(a) any land or other place (whether enclosed or not); and

(b) any outbuildings which are or are used as part of the premises; and

"relevant harm" means—

(a) significant and persistent disorder; or

(b) significant, persistent and serious nuisance to members of the public.

GENERAL NOTE

Although the definition of premises is wide, there are clearly difficulties in applying these provisions to unenclosed land.

PART 5

NOISE NUISANCE

GENERAL NOTE

This part of the Act deals with noise nuisance and complements existing powers under the Civic Government Act 1982 (*e.g.* s.54), Environmental Protection Act 1990 (c.43) (*e.g.* s.80), and the Control of Pollution Act 1974. Unlike most of the existing provisions the existence of a noise nuisance is established by a noise exceeding a fixed limit (which varies according to the time of day) rather than having to establish the existence of a nuisance or that there is reasonable cause for alarm or annoyance (as required, for example, in respect of dangerous or annoying creatures under s.49 of the Civic Government (Scotland) Act 1982 (c.45)). Whether, and the extent to which, these provisions apply to particular areas will be a matter for the local authority to decide.

Since this part of the Act came into force there seems to have been a widespread practice on the part of local authorities of declaring he whole of their area to be covered by its provisions.

Summary procedure for dealing with noise from certain places

Application of noise control provisions to local authority areas

41.—(1) Sections 43 to 47 (the "noise control provisions") apply to the area of a local authority only if the authority has so resolved.

(2) A resolution for the purpose of subsection (1) shall specify—

(a) a date (being a date at least 2 months after the passing of the resolution) on and after which the noise control provisions are to have effect in the area of the authority (the "commencement date"); and

(b) periods of the week during which noise is to be controlled by virtue of those provisions (each such period being a "noise control period").

(3) For the purpose of subsection (2)(b), a resolution may specify—

(a) the whole week as a noise control period; and

(b) different noise control periods for different—

    (i) areas;

    (ii) times of year; or

    (iii) other circumstances.

(4) For the purpose of subsection (2)(b), a week begins on Monday.

(5) If a local authority resolves to apply the noise control provisions to its area, it shall—

(a) cause a notice to be published (in consecutive weeks with the second notice appearing at least a month before the commencement date) in a local newspaper circulating in its area; and

(b) at least a month before the commencement date—

    (i) give a copy of the resolution to the Scottish Ministers; and

    (ii) give a copy of the notice mentioned in paragraph (a) to each local authority whose area adjoins its area.

(6) A notice published under subsection (5)(a) shall—

(a) state that the resolution has been passed;

(b) state the commencement date; and

(c) set out—

    (i) the general effect of the noise control provisions and sections 48, 49 and 51; and

    (ii) the noise control periods specified in the resolution.

(7) Where a local authority is given a notice under subsection (5)(b)(ii), it shall take such steps as it considers necessary for the purpose of making persons in its area aware of the contents of the notice.

DEFINITIONS

"commencement date":	subs.(2)(a)
"noise control period":	subs.(2)(b)
"noise control provisions":	subs.(1)

GENERAL NOTE

Before the provisions of this Part of the Act will apply in a particular area the local authority will need to resolve that they do so following the procedure under this section. Such a resolution must specify the date from which the provisions will apply to the area. As indicated in subs.(3) the provisions need not apply all the time, they may be focussed on a particular period or periods, for example weekends, when noise is a particular problem. The periods when the provisions apply in an area are designated as noise control periods. The same noise control periods need not apply all the time or in all of the local authority.

Once the resolution has been passed subss (5) and (6) sets out the steps that the local authority must take to publicise its provisions.

Revocation or variation of resolution under section 41

42.—(1) A local authority may by resolution—

(a) revoke the resolution made for the purpose of section 41(1);

(b) revoke any noise control period specified in that resolution; or

(c) specify noise control periods—
  (i) in addition to; or
  (ii) in substitution for,
  any such noise control period.

(2) A resolution under subsection (1) shall specify a date (being a date at least 2 months after the passing of the resolution) on which the provision made by the resolution shall come into effect (the "effective date").

(3) If a local authority passes a resolution under subsection (1), it shall—

(a) cause a notice to be published (in consecutive weeks with the second notice appearing at least a month before the effective date) in a local newspaper circulating in its area; and

(b) at least a month before the effective date—
  (i) give a copy of the resolution to the Scottish Ministers; and
  (ii) give a copy of the notice mentioned in paragraph (a) to each local authority whose area adjoins its area.

(4) A notice published under subsection (3)(a) shall—

(a) state that the resolution has been passed;

(b) state the effective date; and

(c) set out the provision made by the resolution.

(5) Where a local authority is given a copy of a notice under subsection (3)(b)(ii), it shall take such steps as it considers necessary for the purpose of making persons in its area aware of the contents of the notice.

DEFINITIONS
"effective date":   subs.(2)
"noise control period":   s.41(2)(b)

GENERAL NOTE
This section allows the authority to revoke a resolution passed under s.41 or to vary the terms of such a resolution, for example by changing the periods during which noise is to be subject to control. The notification and publicity provisions are the same as those for the initial resolution.

Noise control provisions

Investigation of excessive noise from certain places

43.—(1) Where a local authority receives a complaint from an individual that excessive noise is being emitted from relevant property during a noise control period, it shall ensure that an officer of the authority investigates the latter matter.

(2) A complaint under subsection (1) may be made by any means.

(3) If in consequence of an investigation under subsection (1) an officer of a local authority is satisfied that—

(a) noise is being emitted from relevant property (the "offending property") during a noise control period; and

(b) the noise, if it were measured from a relevant place—
    (i) would; or
    (ii) might,
exceed the permitted level,
the officer may serve a notice about the noise under section 44.

(4) For the purposes of subsection (3), it is for the officer of the authority dealing with the particular case—

(a) to decide whether any noise, if it were measured from a relevant place—
    (i) would; or
    (ii) might,
exceed the permitted level; and

(b) for the purposes of that decision to decide—
    (i) from what place to assess the noise; and
    (ii) whether to use any device for measuring the noise.

(5) Where—

(a) a local authority (the "first local authority") receives a complaint under subsection (1); and

(b) the offending property is within the area of another local authority,
the first local authority may act under the noise control provisions as if the offending property were within its area, and accordingly may so act whether or not the noise control provisions apply to the area of the other local authority.

DEFINITIONS
"noise control period":	s.41(2)(b)
"offending property":	subs.(3)(a)
"permitted level":	s.48
"relevant place":	s.53
"relevant property":	s.53

GENERAL NOTE

Subsection (1) imposes a duty of investigation on the local authority following a complaint of excessive noise during a noise control period. The investigation is designed to establish whether the noise exceeds or might exceed the permitted level specified under s.48. Unlike other legislation (referred to under the General Note to this Part) a judgement that the noise level exceeds or might exceed the level is enough to permit action to be taken without further consideration of whether the noise amounts to a nuisance. This action is in the form of service of a notice under s.44.

In assessing the noise level the assessment to be made is as to the noise level if a measurement was taken from a relevant place. A relevant place is defined as premises used as accommodation, including flats and parts of a building *e.g.* an individual room designed to be used as separate accommodation (s.53, the Scottish Ministers have the power to designate further relevant places). The noise to be assessed must be coming from a relevant property, which can be other accommodation, a garden attached to such accommodation or the common areas of a tenement or other group of houses (s.53). As long as the relevant place is within the boundaries of the area covered by a noise control resolution made by the local authority the relevant property need not be, and could, in fact be situated within the boundaries of a neighbouring local authority (subs.(5)).

It is important to note that at this stage all that the local authority officer is asked to do is make their own assessment as to whether, if a measurement was taken, the level of noise inside the relevant place would exceed the permitted noise level. As subs.(4)(b)(ii) makes clear it is not necessary to actually make a measurement of the noise using a noise measuring device.

Warning notices

44.—(1) A notice under this section (a "warning notice") shall—

(a) state that an officer of the authority considers—
    (i) that noise is being emitted from the offending property during a noise control period; and
    (ii) that the noise exceeds, or may exceed, the permitted level, as measured from a relevant place; and
(b) state that any person who is responsible for noise which—
    (i) is emitted from the offending property in the period specified in the notice; and
    (ii) exceeds the permitted level as measured from a relevant place,
may be guilty of an offence.

(2) The period specified in a warning notice shall be a period—
(a) beginning not earlier than 10 minutes after the time when the notice is served; and
(b) ending at the relevant time.

(3) In subsection (2)(b), "relevant time" means the earlier of—
(a) the end of the noise control period during which the warning notice is served; and
(b) the point (if any) at which the permitted level at the time the notice is served ceases to be applicable.

(4) Subject to subsection (5), a warning notice shall be served by delivering it to any person present at or near the offending property and appearing to the officer of the authority to be responsible for the noise.

(5) If it is not reasonably practicable to identify any person present at or near the offending property as being a person responsible for the noise on whom the notice may reasonably be served, a warning notice shall be served by leaving it at the offending property.

(6) A warning notice shall state the time at which it is served.

(7) For the purpose of the noise control provisions, a person is responsible for noise emitted from relevant property if the emission of the noise is wholly or partly attributable to the person's act, failure or sufferance.

DEFINITIONS
"noise control period":	s.41(2)(b)
"offending property":	s.43(3)(a)
"permitted level":	s.48
"relevant place":	s.53
"relevant time":	subs.(3)
"warning notice":	subs.(1)

GENERAL NOTE
Once a local authority officer is satisfied that, if measured from within accommodation, the noise level coming from another property (the offending property) would or might exceed the permitted level a notice can be served under this section. The warning notice indirectly controls the noise level by indicating that exceeding the permitted noise level is an offence. The form and content of the notice and procedure for service are straightforward. The notice takes effect no sooner than ten minutes after service and will end on the happening of one of two events. First, it will come to an end if the noise control period comes to an end. For example, if the noise control period finishes at 6am on Monday morning, a notice served at 2am that morning will end then. Secondly, the notice will come to an end when the permitted noise level changes. The permitted noise level changes at 7am, 7pm and 11pm, so, for example, a notice served at 8pm would cease at 11pm, even though the permitted noise level coming into effect then is lower than that at 8pm, see The Antisocial Behaviour (Noise Control) (Scotland) Regulations 2005 (SSI 2005/43), reg. 3 and Schedule.

Offence where noise exceeds permitted level after service of notice

45.—(1) If a warning notice has been served in respect of noise emitted from relevant property, any person who is responsible for noise which—

(a) is emitted from the relevant property in the period specified in the notice; and

(b) exceeds the permitted level as measured from a relevant place,

shall be guilty of an offence.

(2) A person guilty of an offence under subsection (1) shall be liable on summary conviction to a fine not exceeding level 3 on the standard scale.

(3) It shall be a defence for a person charged with an offence under subsection (1) to show that there was a reasonable excuse for the act, failure or sufferance by reference to which the person was charged.

(4) A person shall be taken to have shown the matter mentioned in subsection (3) if—

(a) sufficient evidence is adduced to raise an issue with respect to it; and

(b) the prosecution does not prove the contrary beyond reasonable doubt.

(5) In proceedings for an offence under this section, a measurement of noise by a device is not admissible as evidence of a level of noise unless the device is an approved device and any conditions subject to which the approval was given are satisfied.

DEFINITIONS

"permitted level":	s.48
"relevant place":	s.53
"relevant property":	s.53
"warning notice":	s.44(1)

GENERAL NOTE

Failure to comply with a warning notice is an offence. A failure to comply will occur when noise coming from the property covered by the notice exceeds the permitted level when measured from within a relevant place (essentially another building or part of a building used as accommodation, see s.53). At this stage, unlike under s.43, there will be a need for a measurement of the noise level and this must be made using a device approved under s.49. On measurement see The Antisocial Behaviour (Noise Control) (Scotland) Regulations 2005 (SSI 2005/43), regs. 6 & 7.

The person committing the offence is the person responsible for the noise. As s.44(7) makes clear, this may involve an act, a failure to act or sufferance of the noise. There may be a defence if that person can show that there was a reasonable excuse for their action or inaction. Once there is a *prima facie* case for the existence of an excuse, the standard of proof that the prosecution has to reach to prove that there was no reasonable excuse is the criminal standard of beyond a reasonable doubt.

Prosecution for breach of the warning notice is only one option, the authority might also take action under the Environmental Protection Act 1990, or there may be a prosecution under s.54 of the Civic Government (Scotland) Act 1982 if it applies in the circumstances. A s.54 offence will be committed where someone (a) sounds or plays any musical instrument; (b) sings or performs; or (c) operates any radio or television receiver, record player, tape-recorder or other sound producing device so as to give any other person reasonable cause for annoyance and fails to desist on being required to do so by a constable in uniform.

Fixed penalty notices

46.—(1) Subject to subsection (3), where a relevant officer has reason to believe that a person—

(a) is committing; or

(b) has just committed,

an offence under section 45, the officer may give that person a notice (a "fixed penalty notice") offering the person the opportunity of discharging any liability to conviction for that offence by payment of a fixed penalty.

(2) In subsection (1), "relevant officer" means—

(a) an officer of the local authority authorised for the purposes of this section; or

(b) a constable.

(3) If a fixed penalty notice is given to a person in respect of noise emitted from relevant property in the period specified in a warning notice, no further fixed penalty notice may be given to that person in respect of noise emitted from the relevant property during that period.

(4) Subject to subsection (5), a fixed penalty notice may be given to a person by delivering the notice to the person.

(5) If it is not reasonably practicable to deliver it to the person, a fixed penalty notice shall be given by leaving the notice, addressed to the person, at the offending property.

(6) A fixed penalty notice shall give such particulars of the circumstances alleged to constitute the offence as are necessary for giving reasonable information of the offence.

(7) A fixed penalty notice shall state—

(a) the period during which, by virtue of paragraph (a) of section 51(2), proceedings will not be taken for the offence;

(b) the amount of the fixed penalty; and

(c) the person to whom, and the address at which, the fixed penalty may be paid.

(8) Payment of the fixed penalty may (among other methods) be made by pre-paying and posting to that person at that address a letter containing the amount of the penalty (in cash or otherwise).

(9) Where a letter containing the amount of the penalty is sent in accordance with subsection (8), payment is to be regarded as having been made at the time at which that letter would be delivered in the ordinary course of post.

(10) The fixed penalty payable under this section is £100.

(11) A fixed penalty payable under this section shall be payable to the local authority whose officer issued the warning notice under reference to which the offence was committed.

DEFINITIONS

"fixed penalty notice":	subs.(1)
"relevant officer":	subs.(2)
"relevant property":	s.53
"warning notice":	s.44(1)

GENERAL NOTE

Where there is a breach of a warning notice served under s.44 either an authorised officer of the local authority or a police officer can serve a fixed penalty notice in respect of the breach. Once a fixed penalty notice has been served a further notice cannot then be served if there is a subsequent breach of the warning notice (though there may be a prosecution for this later breach: s.51(2)(c)). The person served with the notice has 28 days to pay the fixed penalty before a prosecution can be initiated (subs.(7)(a) and s.51(2)).

Powers of entry and seizure of equipment used to make noise unlawfully

47.—(1) Subsection (2) applies where—

(a) a warning notice has been served in respect of noise emitted from relevant property; and

(b) an officer of the local authority in whose area the relevant property is situated has reason to believe that, at any time in the period specified in the notice, noise emitted from the relevant property has exceeded the permitted level as measured from a relevant place.

(2) An officer of the local authority, or a person authorised by the authority for the purpose, may seize and remove any equipment which appears—

(a) to be being; or
(b) to have been,
used in the emission of the noise.

(3) If required to do so, a person exercising the power conferred by subsection (2) shall produce the person's authority.

(4) If a sheriff or justice of the peace is satisfied by evidence on oath—
(a) that a warning notice has been served in respect of noise emitted from relevant property;
(b) that, at any time in the period specified in the notice, noise emitted from the relevant property has exceeded the permitted level, as measured from a relevant place; and
(c) that—
(i) entry of an officer of the local authority, or of a person authorised by the authority for the purpose, to the relevant property has been refused;
(ii) such a refusal is apprehended; or
(iii) a request by an officer of the authority, or of such a person, for admission would defeat the object of the entry,
the sheriff or justice may grant a warrant under this subsection.

(5) A warrant under subsection (4) is a warrant authorising the local authority, by any of its officers or any person authorised by it for the purpose—
(a) to enter the relevant property for the purpose of seizing and removing any equipment which appears to be being used or to have been used in the emission of the noise; and
(b) for the purpose of exercising the power mentioned in paragraph (a), to open lockfast places on the relevant property.

(6) A person who enters premises by virtue of a warrant granted under subsection (4)—
(a) may be accompanied by such persons, and take such equipment, as may be necessary; and
(b) shall, where the relevant property is unoccupied on the person's leaving, leave it as effectively secured against trespassers as it was when the person entered it.

(7) A person who wilfully obstructs a person—
(a) exercising the power conferred by subsection (2); or
(b) exercising the power conferred by a warrant granted under subsection (4),
shall be guilty of an offence.

(8) A person guilty of an offence under subsection (7) shall be liable on summary conviction to a fine not exceeding level 3 on the standard scale.

(9) Schedule 1 (which makes further provision in relation to anything seized and removed by virtue of this section) shall have effect.

DEFINITIONS
"permitted level":	s.48
"relevant property":	s.53
"warning notice":	s.44(1)

GENERAL NOTE
Once a warning notice has been served under s.44 and this is then breached by exceeding the permitted noise levels, the local authority is empowered to seize any equipment used in the emission of the noise causing the breach. If entry to effect such a seizure is refused (which would amount to the offence of obstruction under subs.(7)(a)) a warrant can be obtained to permit entry. Schedule 1 makes further provisions regarding the retention of equipment which

is seized and the power of the court to order forfeiture of this equipment on conviction of an offence under s.45. Where a fixed penalty notice is issued and paid within the time allowed any equipment seized must be returned.

The permitted level

Permitted level of noise
48.—(1) For the purposes of the noise control provisions, the Scottish Ministers may by regulations prescribe the maximum level of noise (the "permitted level") which may be emitted from relevant property.

(2) The permitted level shall be a level for noise as measured from any relevant place by an approved device used in accordance with any conditions subject to which the approval was given.

(3) Different permitted levels may be prescribed for different—
(a) periods of the week;
(b) areas or descriptions of areas;
(c) times of year; or
(d) other circumstances,

and the permitted level may be prescribed partly by reference to other levels of noise.

DEFINITIONS
"relevant property":   s.53

GENERAL NOTE
The permitted noise levels are set out in The Antisocial Behaviour (Noise Control) (Scotland) Regulations 2005 (SSI 2005/43), reg. 3 and Schedule.

Miscellaneous

Approval of measuring devices
49.—(1) For the purposes of the noise control provisions, the Scottish Ministers may by regulations approve any type of device used for the measurement of noise.

(2) An approval under subsection (1) may be given subject to such conditions as to—
(a) the purposes for which; or
(b) the manner and circumstances in which,
    devices of the type approved are to be used as may be prescribed in the regulations.

GENERAL NOTE
See The Antisocial Behaviour (Noise Control) (Scotland) Regulations 2005 (SSI 2005/43) for details of approved devices.

Power to provide funds to local authorities
50.—(1) The Scottish Ministers may make to a local authority payments in respect of—
(a) the whole; or
(b) any part,
    of the expenditure of the authority in relation to the discharge of the functions under this Part of the authority and its officers.

(2) Payments under this section shall be made at such times, in such manner and subject to such conditions as the Scottish Ministers may determine.

It is clear from a survey conducted shortly before the passing of the Act that different authorities operate very different levels of service in respect of antisocial noise, see *Guidance on Noise Nuisance*. This section is designed to permit the provision of additional funds to finance additional services to make use of the new powers contained in this Part of the Act.

Fixed penalty notices: supplementary

51.—(1) If a form for a fixed penalty notice is specified in an order made by the Scottish Ministers, a fixed penalty notice shall be given in that form.

(2) Where a person is given a fixed penalty notice—

(a) proceedings for the offence in respect of which the notice was given shall not be instituted before the end of the period of 28 days beginning with the date of the notice;

(b) the person cannot be convicted of that offence if the person pays the fixed penalty before the end of that period; and

(c) the person may be convicted of a further offence under section 45 in respect of noise emitted from the relevant property—

(i) after the notice is given; and

(ii) before the end of the period specified in the warning notice.

(3) In proceedings for an offence under section 45, evidence that payment of a fixed penalty was or was not made before the end of any period may be given by the production of a certificate which—

(a) purports to be signed by or on behalf of the person having responsibility for the financial affairs of the local authority; and

(b) states that payment of a fixed penalty was made on any date or, as the case may be, was not received before the end of that period.

(4) Subject to subsection (5), the Scottish Ministers may by order amend section 46(10) by substituting an amount specified in the order for the amount that is for the time being mentioned in that section.

(5) The Scottish Ministers may not specify an amount exceeding level 2 on the standard scale.

(6) Any sum received by a local authority under section 46 shall be treated as if the fixed penalty payable under that section were a fine imposed by a district court.

DEFINITIONS
"fixed penalty notice":   s.46(1)

Guidance in relation to this Part

52.—A person (other than a court) shall, in discharging functions by virtue of this Part, have regard to any guidance given by the Scottish Ministers about—

(a) the discharge of those functions; and

(b) matters arising in connection with the discharge of those functions.

The *Guidance on Noise Nuisance* can be found at: http://www.scotland.gov.uk/library5/social/asbn.pdf

Interpretation

Meaning of "relevant place" and "relevant property"

53.—(1) In this Part—

"relevant place" means—

(a) any place within accommodation (except, in the case of measurement of noise emitted from relevant property which is accommodation, that accommodation); and

(b) such other place as may be prescribed;
"relevant property" means—
(a) any accommodation;
(b) any land belonging exclusively to, or enjoyed exclusively with, any accommodation;
(c) any land not falling within paragraph (b)—
  (i) to which at least two persons have rights in common; and
  (ii) which is used by those persons as a private garden;
(d) any common passage, close, court, stair, lift or yard pertinent to any tenement or group of separately owned houses; or
(e) such other place as may be prescribed.
(2) In subsection (1)—
"accommodation" means a building or other structure (or part of a building or other structure) used or intended to be used as a separate unit of accommodation (whether on a permanent basis or otherwise); and
"prescribed" means prescribed by the Scottish Ministers by order.

Interpretation of Part 5
54.—(1) In this Part—
"fixed penalty notice" has the meaning given by section 46(1);
"noise control period" has the meaning given by section 41(2)(b);
"noise control provisions" has the meaning given by section 41(1);
"offending property" has the meaning given by section 43(3)(a);
"permitted level" has the meaning given by section 48(1); and
"warning notice" has the meaning given by section 44(1).
(2) References in this Part to approved devices are references to devices of a type approved by virtue of section 49(1).

PART 6

THE ENVIRONMENT

Controlled waste and litter

Contraventions of section 33(1)(a) and (c) of 1990 Act: fixed penalty notices
55. After section 33 of the Environmental Protection Act 1990 (c.43) ("the 1990 Act") there shall be inserted—
"**Fixed penalty notices for contraventions of section 33(1)(a) and (c): Scotland**
33A.—(1) Where—
(a) an authorised officer of a local authority has reason to believe that a person has committed a relevant offence in the area of that authority; or
(b) a constable, or an authorised officer of a waste regulation authority, has reason to believe that a person has committed a relevant offence,
he may give that person a notice under this section in respect of the offence.
(2) In subsection (1) above, "relevant offence" means an offence under section 33 above in respect of a contravention of subsection (1)(a) or (c) of that section.
(3) A notice under this section is a notice offering the opportunity, by paying a fixed penalty, of discharging any liability to conviction for the offence to which it relates.

(4) Where—

(a) a constable; or

(b) an authorised officer of a waste regulation authority,

gives a notice under this section to a person, he shall, no later than 24 hours after the giving of the notice, send a copy of it to the local authority in whose area the offence was committed.

(5) Where a person is given a notice under this section in respect of an offence—

(a) no proceedings shall be instituted for that offence before the expiration of fourteen days following the date of the notice; and

(b) he shall not be convicted of that offence if he pays the fixed penalty before the expiration of that period.

(6) A notice under this section shall give such particulars of the circumstances alleged to constitute the offence as are necessary for giving reasonable information about the offence and shall state—

(a) the period during which, by virtue of subsection (5)(a) above, proceedings will not be taken for the offence;

(b) the amount of the fixed penalty; and

(c) the person to whom and the address at which the fixed penalty may be paid;

and without prejudice to payment by any other method, payment of the fixed penalty may be made by pre-paying and posting to that person at that address a letter containing the amount of the penalty (in cash or otherwise).

(7) Where a letter is sent in accordance with subsection (6) above payment shall be regarded as having been made at the time at which that letter would be delivered in the ordinary course of post.

(8) The form of notices under this section shall be such as the Scottish Ministers may by order prescribe.

(9) The fixed penalty payable in pursuance of a notice under this section shall, subject to subsection (10) below, be £50.

(10) The Scottish Ministers may by order substitute a different amount (not exceeding level 2 on the standard scale) for the amount for the time being specified as the amount of the fixed penalty in subsection (9) above.

(11) In any proceedings a certificate which—

(a) purports to be signed by or on behalf of the proper officer for the local authority in whose area the offence was committed; and

(b) states that the payment of a fixed penalty was or was not received by a date specified in the certificate,

shall be evidence of the facts stated.

(12) A fixed penalty payable in pursuance of a notice under this section shall be payable to the local authority in whose area the offence was committed; and as respects the sums received by a local authority, those sums shall be treated as if the penalty were a fine imposed by a district court.

(13) In this section—

"authorised officer" means an officer of the authority in question who is authorised in writing by the authority for the purpose of issuing notices under this section;

"local authority" means a council constituted under section 2 of the Local Government etc. (Scotland) Act 1994 (c.39); and "area", in relation to a local authority, means the local government area (within the meaning of that Act) for which the council is constituted;

"proper officer" means the officer who has, as respects the authority, the responsibility mentioned in section 95 of the Local Government (Scotland) Act 1973 (c.65) (financial administration).".

GENERAL NOTE

The offences in the Environmental Protection Act 1990 which are referred to here involve the treatment, deposit, disposal or keeping of controlled waste. The effect of the section is to introduce a new fixed penalty notice to address these offences. The period for payment of the notice is short (14 days, subs.(5)(a)), and in comparison to the maximum penalties payable on conviction the amount of the fixed penalty is low. See The Controlled Waste (Fixed Penalty Notices) (Scotland) Order 2004 (SSI 2004/426) for the form of notice.

Litter: power of constables to issue fixed penalty notices

56.—(1) Section 88 of the 1990 Act (fixed penalty notices for litter) shall be amended as follows.

(2) In subsection (1)—

(a) the words "on any occasion" and "finds a person who he" shall be repealed;

(b) for "has on that occasion" there shall be substituted "that a person has";

(c) the words from "an", where it first occurs, to "authority", where it secondly occurs, shall become paragraph (a) of that subsection; and

(d) after "authority", where it secondly occurs, there shall be inserted "; or

(b) a constable has reason to believe that a person has committed an offence under that section,".

(3) After subsection (1) there shall be inserted—

"(1A) Where a constable gives a notice under this section to a person, he shall, no later than 24 hours after the giving of the notice, send a copy of it to the litter authority in whose area the offence was committed.".

(4) After subsection (5) there shall be inserted—

"(5A) A fixed penalty payable in pursuance of a notice under this section shall be payable to the litter authority in whose area the offence was committed.".

(5) In subsection (6)—

(a) the words "to a litter authority" are repealed; and

(b) for "the", where it thirdly occurs, there shall be substituted "a litter".

(6) In subsection (7), after "amount", where it first occurs, there shall be inserted "(not exceeding level 2 on the standard scale)".

(7) In subsection (8)(a)(ii), after "officer" there shall be inserted "for the litter authority in whose area the offence was committed".

GENERAL NOTE

The effect of this section is to empower police officers to serve a fixed penalty notice for littering offences. Section 88 as originally enacted only conferred this power on local authority officers. There is also some tidying up of the wording of the section. See The Litter (Fixed Penalty Notices) (Scotland) Order 2004 (SSI 2004/427) for the form of notice.

Directions in respect of duty under section 89 of 1990 Act

57.—(1) Sections 89, 91 and 92 of the 1990 Act shall be amended as follows.

(2) In section 89 (duties to keep land etc. free of litter), after subsection (6) there shall be inserted—

"(6A) The Scottish Ministers may give to any person subject to a duty imposed by subsection (1) or (2) above such directions as they consider necessary or expedient for securing compliance by such person with such duty.

(6B) A person to whom a direction is given under subsection (6A) shall comply with the direction.

(6C) A direction under subsection (6A) may—
  (a) be given generally or to a specific person;
  (b) make different provision for different persons and different cases or circumstances;
  (c) include provision specifying, in relation to any factor by reference to which a person's discharging of any such duty can be measured, standards to be met by the person.

(6D) The Scottish Ministers shall—
  (a) cause—
       (i) any direction under subsection (6A) above; and
      (ii) any variation or revocation of such a direction,
       to be published; and
  (b) cause copies of each such direction, variation or revocation to be made available to the public.".

(3) In section 91 (litter abatement orders: applications by aggrieved persons), in subsection (11)—
  (a) after "A", where it first occurs, there shall be inserted—
      "(a) direction under section 89(6A); or";
  (b) the words "code of practice under section 89(7)" shall become paragraph (b); and
  (c) after "a", where it secondly occurs, there shall be inserted "direction or".

(4) In section 92 (litter abatement notices: litter authorities), in subsection (8)—
  (a) after "A", where it first occurs, there shall be inserted—
      "(a) direction under section 89(6A); or";
  (b) the words "code of practice under section 89(7)" shall become paragraph (b); and
  (c) after "a", where it secondly occurs, there shall be inserted "direction or".

GENERAL NOTE
These amendments give the Scottish Ministers a new power to give directions to a variety of bodies regarding compliance with their obligation to ensure that their land is kept clear of litter and refuse. The directions can be given to, amongst others, local authorities, statutory undertakers, and educational institutions.

Graffiti

Power of local authority to serve notice about graffiti
    58.—(1) Where it appears to a local authority that—
  (a) a relevant surface in its area has been defaced by graffiti; and
  (b) the defacement is—
       (i) detrimental to the amenity of the locality; or
      (ii) offensive,
       the authority may serve a graffiti removal notice on any responsible person.

(2) A graffiti removal notice is a notice requiring the person on whom it is served to remove, clear or otherwise remedy the defacement described in the notice before the expiry of such period as may be specified in the notice (being a period of not less than 28 days beginning with the day on which the notice is served).

(3) A relevant surface is—
(a) any surface of—
   (i) a public road; or
   (ii) any building, structure, apparatus, plant or other object on such a road; or
(b) where subsection (4) or (5) applies, any surface of—
   (i) land owned, occupied or controlled by a relevant body; or
   (ii) any building, structure, apparatus, plant or other object on such land.
(4) This subsection applies where the land is public land.
(5) This subsection applies where—
(a) the surface is visible from public land; or
(b) the surface is not visible from public land but is visible to members of the public from land owned, occupied or controlled by—
   (i) the relevant body which owns, occupies or controls the land; or
   (ii) any other relevant body,
   which they are on for the purpose of using that body's services or facilities.
(6) For the purposes of this section, a road or land is public if the public are entitled or permitted to have access to it (with or without payment).
(7) A local authority may at any time withdraw a graffiti removal notice issued by it.
(8) The withdrawal, under subsection (7), of a graffiti removal notice (the "withdrawn notice") shall not affect the power of the local authority to issue a further graffiti removal notice in respect of the defacement described in the withdrawn notice.
(9) In this section—
   "educational institution" has the meaning given by section 98(3) of the 1990 Act and includes the governing body of such an institution;
   "graffiti" includes painting, writing, soiling, marking or otherwise defacing by whatever means;
   "relevant body" means—
     (a) an educational institution; or
     (b) a statutory undertaker;
   "responsible person" means, in relation to a surface, a person who owns, leases, occupies, controls, operates or maintains the thing of which it is a surface;
   "road" has the meaning given by section 151(1) of the Roads (Scotland) Act 1984 (c.54);
   "statutory undertaker" has the meaning given by section 98(6) of the 1990 Act; and
   "surface" includes a surface—
     (a) on the inside of a thing; or
     (b) not exposed to the weather.

DEFINITIONS

"educational institution":	subs.(9)
"graffiti":	subs.(9)
"graffiti removal notice":	subs.(2)
"relevant body":	subs.(9)
"relevant surface":	subs.(3)
"responsible person":	subs.(9)
"road":	subs.(9)
"statutory undertaker":	subs.(9)
"surface":	subs.(9)

The simple objective of this rather complicated section is to give the local authority the power to require the removal of certain types of graffiti. This power can only be exercised where the surface covered in graffiti is either on a public road or where it belongs either to an educational institution or to a statutory undertaker. A surface will be on a public road if it is either the surface of the road itself or if it is on something physically placed on the road or on a pavement. The main examples are the boxes used by various companies, for example cable television providers. Walls alongside a road will, perhaps despite normal parlance to the contrary, not be on the road, rather they are adjacent to the road and so, subject to the exceptions noted below, not covered by this provision.

Statutory undertakers are, for the purposes of this section, transport operators, such as rail operators or harbour undertakings (Environmental Protection Act 1990, s.98(6)). Only certain surfaces owned by these undertakings or by educational institutions are covered. In summary they are as follows:

   (i)   The surface of any land or structure on land where the land is public in the sense that the public are entitled to access to it, whether they have to pay for this access or not.

  (ii)   Surfaces which are visible from public land, *e.g.* the surface of a railway bridge which is visible from a public park.

 (iii)   Surfaces visible to members of the public who are land belonging to the same or another undertaker or institution to use services or facilities provided by that undertaker or institution. This would cover, for example, surfaces of walls in a school visible to pupils and the surface of a wall only visible to train passengers.

Provided that graffiti is on a surface which falls within one of these categories a notice requiring its removal can only be served if either the graffiti is offensive, *e.g.* racially or sexually offensive, or where it is detrimental to the amenity of the locality. This last limitation indicates that it will not be competent to serve a notice where the removal of graffiti would have little effect on the amenity of an area. For example, if there was a cable box covered with graffiti directly in front of a privately owned wall similarly covered, the local authority would only have power to require removal of the graffiti on the box and that removal would have very little impact.

The guidance, *Guidance on Graffiti Removal*, suggests that there should be consultation with the person responsible for the surface before a notice is served and this might include discussion of the period for compliance with the notice (subs.(3) only specifies a minimum period). There is a right of appeal against service of a notice (s.63).

Power to modify meaning of "relevant surface"

59.—(1) The Scottish Ministers may by order modify—

(a) paragraph (a) or (b) of subsection (3); or

(b) subsection (4), (5) or (6),

of section 58.

(2) An order under subsection (1) may make such modifications of subsection (9) of that section as the Scottish Ministers consider appropriate in consequence of any modification made by virtue of subsection (1).

Graffiti removal notice: content and service

60.—(1) A graffiti removal notice shall explain the effects of sections 61, 63 and 64.

(2) Subject to subsection (3), subsections (2) to (5) of section 160 of the 1990 Act shall apply in relation to the service of a graffiti removal notice as they apply to any notice required or authorised to be served under that Act.

(3) Where, after reasonable enquiry, a local authority is unable to ascertain the name or proper address of any person upon whom a graffiti removal notice may be served, it may—

(a) affix the notice to the surface to which it relates; and

(b) in so far as is reasonably necessary for that purpose, enter any land.

(4) In subsection (3), "proper address" shall be read in accordance with section 160(4) and (5) of the 1990 Act.

(5) Where a graffiti removal notice is affixed in accordance with subsection (3), it shall be treated as having been served on a person on whom it may be served.

DEFINITIONS
"graffiti removal notice":   s.58(2)

GENERAL NOTE
   This sets out the required content of a graffiti removal notice and the requirements for service.

Non-compliance with graffiti removal notice

61.—(1) Subsection (2) applies where a person on whom a graffiti removal notice is served (the "responsible person") does not comply with it.
   (2) The local authority that served the notice or a person authorised by it may—
   (a) remove, clear or otherwise remedy the defacement; and
   (b) in so far as is reasonably necessary for that purpose, enter any land.
   (3) Where subsection (4) applies, a local authority may recover from the responsible person expenditure reasonably incurred by virtue of subsection (2).
   (4) This subsection applies where the local authority has served on the responsible person a notice setting out—
   (a) the amount of; and
   (b) details of,
      the expenditure which it proposes to recover.
   (5) Subsections (2) to (5) of section 160 of the 1990 Act shall apply in relation to the service of a notice mentioned in subsection (4) as they apply to notices required or authorised to be served under that Act.

DEFINITIONS
"graffiti removal notice":   s.58(2)
"responsible person":   subs.(1)

GENERAL NOTE
   In the event that a graffiti removal notice is not complied with the local authority is empowered to have the work carried out and recover its costs. Where recovery of costs is sought the person required to pay can appeal under s.64. The *Guidance on Graffiti Removal* notes that caution will have to be exercised, for example, in cleaning cable boxes where cleaning fluid may be able to enter the box and damage the contents. Although s.65 confers an exemption from liability on local authorities for work carried out under this section, this will not apply where there has been a failure to exercise due care and attention (s.65(3)(b)).

Guidance to local authorities about graffiti removal functions

62. A local authority shall, in discharging its functions under sections 58, 60 and 61, have regard to any guidance about those sections given by the Scottish Ministers.

GENERAL NOTE
   The *Guidance on Graffiti Removal* can be found at: http://www.scotland.gov.uk/library5/social/asbgr.pdf

Appeal against graffiti removal notice

63.—(1) On the application of a person on whom a graffiti removal notice is served, the sheriff may—
   (a) if satisfied that—
      (i) the surface to which the notice relates was not, at the time the notice was served, defaced as described in it;
      (ii) the defacement described in the notice is neither detrimental to the amenity of the locality nor offensive; or

(iii) the applicant was not, at the time the notice was served, a responsible person as respects the surface to which the notice relates,

make an order revoking the notice; or

(b) if satisfied that there is a material defect in, or in connection with, the notice, make an order revoking or (if appropriate) amending the notice.

(2) In subsection (1)(a)(iii), "responsible person" has the same meaning as in section 58.

(3) Where a sheriff—

(a) makes an order under paragraph (b) of subsection (1) amending a graffiti removal notice; or

(b) makes an order refusing an application such as is mentioned in that subsection,

the sheriff may extend (for such period as may be specified in the order) the period specified in the notice.

(4) An application such as is mentioned in subsection (1) shall be made before the expiry of the period of 21 days beginning with the day on which the graffiti removal notice to which it relates was served.

(5) Where an application such as is mentioned in subsection (1) is made, the graffiti removal notice to which it relates shall be of no effect pending the—

(a) determination; or

(b) withdrawal,

of the application.

DEFINITIONS

"graffiti removal notice":   s.58(2)
"responsible person":   s.58(9)

GENERAL NOTE

The person on whom a graffiti removal notice is served has 21 days to appeal against it. The sheriff can only revoke the order if he/she is satisfied as to one of the grounds in subs.(1)(a). Subsection (1)(a)(ii) suggests the possibility of interesting debates on what is detrimental to amenity in an area. Where there is a defect in the notice or in connection with the notice the sheriff has the power either to revoke or to amend the notice. Pending resolution of the appeal the order is suspended (subs.(5)).

Appeal against notice under section 61(4)

64.—(1) On the application of a person on whom a notice under section 61(4) is served, the sheriff may, if satisfied that the expenditure which the authority is proposing to recover is excessive, make an order substituting for that amount a lower one.

(2) An application such as is mentioned in subsection (1) shall be made within the period of 21 days beginning with the day on which the notice to which it relates was served.

Graffiti removal notice: exemptions from liability

65.—(1) Subject to subsection (3), a relevant person shall have no liability whatsoever (whether at common law or otherwise) to any responsible person in respect of anything done or omitted to be done in the exercise or purported exercise of the power conferred by section 60(3) or 61(2).

(2) In subsection (1), "relevant person" means—

(a) in the case of the power conferred by section 60(3)—

(i) the local authority; and
(ii) any employee of the authority;
(b) in the case of the power conferred by section 61(2)—
(i) the local authority;
(ii) any employee of the authority;
(iii) any person authorised by the authority under that section; and
(iv) any employer or employee of a person so authorised.
(3) Subsection (1) does not apply—
(a) if the act or omission is shown to have been in bad faith; or
(b) in respect of a liability arising out of a failure to exercise due care and attention.
(4) In this section, "responsible person" has the same meaning as in section 58.
(5) This section is without prejudice to any other exemption from liability (whether at common law or otherwise).

DEFINITIONS
"relevant person":   subs.(2)

GENERAL NOTE
Local authorities have an exemption from liability from anything done in respect of service of a graffiti removal notice by attaching it to property or entry to land to serve a notice. This exemption is extended to those authorised by the authority to carry out removal of graffiti where a notice is not complied with. The exemption does not extend to anything done in bad faith or to a failure to exercise due care and attention (subs.(3)).

Penalties for environmental offences

Increase in penalties for certain environmental offences

66. Schedule 2 (which contains amendments relating to penalties for certain environmental offences) shall have effect.

Interpretation

Interpretation of Part 6

67. In this Part, "the 1990 Act" means the Environmental Protection Act 1990 (c.43).

PART 7

HOUSING: ANTISOCIAL BEHAVIOUR NOTICES

GENERAL NOTE
This part is designed to tackle problems of antisocial behaviour by tenants in the private sector. It provides for the local authority to serve a notice on a private sector landlord requiring that landlord to take steps specified in the notice to reduce antisocial behaviour by individuals occupying or visiting property owned by the landlord (s.68). Failure to comply with the notice is a criminal offence (s.79) as well as enabling the authority to take further action by way of an order suspending rental payments (s.71) or by taking over the management and control of the property (s.74).
The provisions cover not only tenancy agreements, but also agreements which allow the occupation of property which would not met the criteria in Scots law for a tenancy, see General Note to s.68.

Antisocial behaviour notices

Antisocial behaviour notices

68.—(1) Where it appears to a local authority that either person mentioned in subsection (2) is engaging in antisocial behaviour at, or in the locality of, a relevant house situated within the authority's area, the authority may serve an antisocial behaviour notice on the landlord of the relevant house.

(2) Those persons are—

(a) any person who, by virtue of a tenancy or an occupancy arrangement, occupies the relevant house mentioned in subsection (1); and

(b) any visitor for the time being in that house.

(3) An antisocial behaviour notice is a notice—

(a) describing the antisocial behaviour that has been engaged in at, or in the locality of, the relevant house to which the notice relates by either of the persons mentioned in subsection (2);

(b) requiring the landlord of the relevant house to take, before the expiry of such period as may be specified in the notice, such action for the purpose of dealing with the antisocial behaviour as may be so specified;

(c) stating the consequences of failure to take, within that period, the action so specified; and

(d) informing the landlord of the right to request a review under section 69(1).

(4) If the local authority is aware of the name and address of a person who acts for the landlord as respects the tenancy or occupancy arrangement relating to the relevant house, the authority shall, in addition to serving a notice on the landlord under subsection (1), give a copy of the notice to the person.

(5) If—

(a) the local authority is unable to identify the landlord, it may serve the notice under subsection (1) by publishing it in two or more newspapers (of which one shall, if practicable, be a local newspaper) circulating in the locality of the relevant house;

(b) the local authority is aware of the landlord's identity but is unable to ascertain the landlord's current address, it may serve the notice under that subsection by serving it on the landlord—

(i) at the relevant house; and

(ii) if it is aware of a previous address of the landlord, at that address.

(6) For the purpose of applying this Part in relation to relevant houses which are used for holiday purposes, the Scottish Ministers may by order make such modifications of the Part as they consider necessary or expedient.

DEFINITIONS

"antisocial behaviour:	s.81(4)
"landlord":	s.81(1)
"occupancy arrangement":	s.81(1)
"relevant house":	s.81(1)

GENERAL NOTE

Where someone occupying premises in the private sector either under a tenancy or other occupancy agreement, or someone visiting a house occupied under one of these arrangements, behaves in an antisocial manner a notice can be served on their landlord. This notice will require the landlord to take certain specified action to address the antisocial behaviour. There are several points in this in need some further explanation.

The scope of the provision is wide, it covers not only tenancy arrangements, but also any other arrangement by which someone is allowed to occupy property, whether or not there is a contract allowing them to do so. Thus it would cover premises occupied under a licence whether or not this had been formally agreed. For a discussion of the requirements for a tenancy and of different forms of entitlement to occupy premises see A McAllister, *The Scottish Law of* Leases (3rd ed. 2002), paras 1.1–1.11 and Ch.2). It also covers, in its definition of relevant house, any part of a building, though where separately occupied rooms share toilet, washing or cooking facilities the whole will be regarded as the relevant house. The scope of these definitions is enough to include privately run hostels and so-called bed and breakfast establishments whose concern is not with holidaymakers. Premises with a resident landlord will also be included. Subsection (6) permits modification of the provisions in respect of holiday accommodation.

Antisocial behaviour for the purposes of this part of the Act is wider than the general definition contained in s.140 as it includes behaviour which causes annoyance or nuisance in addition to alarm and distress.

The content and procedure for service of a notice are set out in subss (3)—(5). Subsection (4) refers to the requirement to serve a copy of the notice on someone who acts for the landlord, this phrase was introduced at Stage 3 to replace references to the landlord's agent as this term was considered to have a technical legal meaning which might not cover all of those on whom a notice should be served.

Review of antisocial behaviour notices

69.—(1) If a landlord on whom an antisocial behaviour notice is served under section 68(1) requests the local authority that served the notice to review the notice, the local authority shall review the notice.

(2) A request under subsection (1) shall be made before the expiry of the period of 21 days beginning with the day on which the notice is served or such longer period as the authority may allow.

(3) There is no duty to carry out a review of a decision reached on review.

DEFINITIONS
"antisocial behaviour notice":   s.68(1)

GENERAL NOTE
There is no right of appeal against service of a notice, rather the landlord can ask the local authority to review the notice. Once a notice has been reviewed once there is no obligation on the authority to review it subsequently on the request of the landlord. The procedure to be followed on review is set out in s.70.

Internal procedure on review

70.—(1) A review of an antisocial behaviour notice under section 69(1) shall be carried out by a person (a "reviewer") who had no involvement in the decision to issue the notice and who is senior to the person who was responsible for the processes culminating in that decision.

(2) The reviewer may—
(a) confirm the notice;
(b) vary any part of it;
(c) suspend the notice for such period as may be specified pending completion of the review; or
(d) revoke the notice.

(3) The local authority shall notify the person who requested the review of the decision reached on review and the reasons for reaching that decision.

DEFINITIONS
"antisocial behaviour notice":   s.68(1)

GENERAL NOTE
The person who reviews an antisocial behaviour notice must have had no involvement in

deciding to issue the notice and must be senior to the person responsible for the issue. The reviewer has extensive powers to vary or revoke the order.

Failure to comply with notice: sanctions

Failure to comply with notice: order as to rental income
71.—(1) If, on the application of the local authority that served an antisocial behaviour notice on a landlord under section 68(1), the sheriff is satisfied as to the matters mentioned in subsection (2), the sheriff may—
  (a) make an order that, with effect from the making of the order—
    (i) no rent be payable by any person who occupies the relevant house; and
    (ii) no other consideration be payable or exigible for occupation of the relevant house; and
  (b) make such incidental order as the sheriff considers necessary.
(2) Those matters are—
  (a) that the landlord has not taken the action specified in the antisocial behaviour notice within the time so specified; and
  (b) that, having regard to all the circumstances relating to the relevant house, it would be reasonable for the landlord to take that action.
(3) Where an order is made under subsection (1), the local authority shall give a copy of the order to the persons mentioned in subsection (4).
(4) Those persons are—
  (a) if the local authority is aware of the name and address of a person who by virtue of a tenancy or an occupancy arrangement occupies the house to which the order relates, that person; and
  (b) if the local authority is aware of the name and address of a person who acts for the landlord as respects the tenancy or occupancy arrangement relating to the relevant house, that person.
(5) Except as provided in an order under subsection (1), nothing in this Part affects the validity of any lease or occupancy arrangement by virtue of which a person has the use of a relevant house during the period when the order is in force.

DEFINITIONS
"antisocial behaviour notice": s.68(1)
"landlord": s.81(1)
"relevant house": s.81(1)

GENERAL NOTE
  Where a landlord fails to take the steps set out in an antisocial behaviour notice the local authority has two remedies. The first is set out in this section, it can apply to the sheriff for an order suspending payment of any rent or other payment due to the landlord by the person occupying accommodation covered by the notice. The sheriff can only make the order if satisfied that it would be reasonable for the landlord to take the action specified in the antisocial behaviour notice. If an order is made it has no effect on the security of tenure or legal rights to occupy of the person occupying the house. Notification requirements are imposed on the local authority in subss (3) and (4).
  Provision is made for appeal against the making or refusal of an order (s.72) and for revocation or suspension of the order (s.73).

Appeals against orders under section 71
72.—(1) An appeal against the decision of a sheriff making or refusing to make an order under section 71(1) shall be made to the sheriff principal and shall be made within the period of 21 days beginning with the day on which the decision appealed against was made.

(2) Subsection (3) applies where a person appeals against the decision of a sheriff making an order under section 71(1)(a).

(3) The person shall (in addition to complying with any other requirements as to notification imposed by virtue of any enactment) give notice to the person who has the use of the house to which the order relates (the "tenant") of such matters as may be prescribed by the Scottish Ministers by regulations.

(4) Regulations under subsection (3) may include provision for or in connection with—

(a) the form of the notice;

(b) the manner and timing of service of the notice.

(5) If a person fails to comply with subsection (3), the sheriff principal shall not require the tenant to pay any sums that, but for the making of the order, would have been due by the tenant.

(6) The Scottish Ministers may by regulations make provision for or in connection with specifying other circumstances in which the sheriff principal shall not require a tenant to pay any sums that, but for the making of the order, would have been due by the tenant.

(7) Regulations under subsection (6) may in particular include provision—

(a) specifying procedures;

(b) imposing obligations on landlords.

(8) The decision of the sheriff principal on an appeal under this section shall be final.

GENERAL NOTE

There is a right to appeal both against the making of an order under s.71 and against a refusal to make an order. Appeal is to the sheriff principal and no further. If an appeal is successful the tenant or occupier will become liable for back rent covering the period from the making of the order. In order to protect the tenant subs.(5) provides that an order for payment of back rent cannot be made where the tenant or occupier has not been notified of the appeal under subs.(3). Some additional protection for tenants is offered by subs.(6). During the stage 3 debate it was suggested that regulations might require the landlord to make a suspense account available to the tenant/occupier into which sums due could be paid pending resolution of the appeal. Failure to make such an account available would prevent an order being made requiring the payment of back rent (Official Report, June 17, 2004, cols 9291–9292).

Orders under section 71: revocation and suspension

73.—(1) This section applies where an order is made under section 71.

(2) On the application of the local authority specified in the order or the landlord of the relevant house which is subject to the order, the sheriff may, if satisfied that—

(a) the landlord has taken the action specified in the antisocial behaviour notice; or

(b) having regard to all the circumstances relating to the relevant house, it would be unreasonable for the order to continue to have effect,

revoke or, for such period as may be specified, suspend the order.

(3) The revocation or suspension of an order under subsection (2) shall not operate so as to make a person liable to pay any rent or other consideration in respect of the period during which the order was in force.

(4) Where an order is revoked or suspended under subsection (2), the local authority shall give a copy of the order revoking or, as the case may be, suspending the order to the persons mentioned in section 71(4).

GENERAL NOTE

Either the landlord or the local authority can apply for revocation or suspension of an order made under s.71. The grounds for revocation or suspension are either that the landlord has complied with the antisocial behaviour notice or that, in all the circumstances, it would be unreasonable for the s.71 order to continue in place. If the order is revoked or suspended the person occupying the house affected by the order will have to start paying rent or whatever sums are due in respect of that occupation, but there will be no liability to make any payment for the period between the making of the order and revocation or suspension.

Failure to comply with notice: management control order

74.—(1) If, on the application of the local authority that served an antisocial behaviour notice on a landlord under section 68(1), the sheriff is satisfied as to the matters mentioned in subsection (2), the sheriff may make a management control order in respect of the house to which the notice relates.

(2) Those matters are—

(a) that the landlord has not taken the action specified in the antisocial behaviour notice within the time so specified;

(b) that, having regard to all the circumstances relating to the relevant house, it would be reasonable for the landlord to take that action; and

(c) that, to enable the antisocial behaviour described in the notice to be dealt with, it is necessary to make the order.

(3) A management control order is an order which—

(a) transfers, for such period not exceeding 12 months as may be specified in the order, to the local authority which made the application the rights and obligations of the landlord under the tenancy or occupancy arrangement under which the house is occupied;

(b) if during that period a tenancy is granted or an occupancy arrangement made for the occupation of the house, transfers for that period to the local authority the rights and obligations of the landlord under that tenancy or arrangement;

(c) makes for that period such incidental provision as the sheriff considers necessary.

(4) Where the local authority on whose application a management control order is made is satisfied that—

(a) sums in respect of rent or other consideration for occupation have been paid to the landlord under the tenancy or occupancy arrangement under which the house is occupied; and

(b) those sums have been paid in respect of a period during which the order is in force,

the authority may recover those sums from the landlord.

(5) Schedule 3 (which makes further provision in relation to management control orders) shall have effect.

DEFINITIONS

"antisocial behaviour notice":	s.68(1)
"landlord":	s.81(1)
"management control order":	subs.(3)
"occupancy arrangement":	s.81(1)

GENERAL NOTE

A second remedy for non-compliance with an antisocial behaviour notice is set out in this section. A management control order can be made in favour of the local authority, transferring the management and control of the house affected to the local authority for a period of up to twelve months. The grounds for making an order are in part the same as the grounds for making an order suspending payment of rent, in other words failure by the landlord to comply with the notice where compliance is reasonable, with the additional requirement that the order is necessary to allow the antisocial behaviour referred to in the notice to be dealt with. The authority can recover any payments made to the landlord while the order is in force (subs(4)). Further provision for management control orders is made is Sch.3, which provides, for example, that the making of the order has no effect on the legal position of the person occupying the house and requires the local authority to keep accounts.

Management control order: notification

75.—(1) Subsection (2) applies where a management control order is made under section 74.

(2) As soon as practicable after the order is made, the local authority on whose application the order was made shall—
  (a) inform—
    (i) the person who, immediately before the order was made, was the landlord of the house to which the order relates; and
    (ii) if the authority is aware of the name and address of a person occupying the house by virtue of a tenancy or occupancy arrangement, that person,
of the making of the order; and
  (b) if the authority is aware of the name and address of a person who acts for the person mentioned in paragraph (a)(i) as respects a tenancy or occupancy arrangement in respect of the house, give a copy of the order to that person.

(3) If it is impracticable for the local authority to comply with the requirement in subsection (2)(a)(i), the authority need not do so.

DEFINITIONS
"landlord": s.81(1)
"management control order": s.74(3)
"occupancy arrangement": s.81(1)

GENERAL NOTE
  This section sets out the parties to whom notification must be made when a management control order has been made. There is no need to notify the landlord if this is impracticable (subs.(3)). Nor will the fact that the authority is not aware of the identity of the occupant affect the validity of an order (subs.(2)(a)(ii)).

Management control order: revocation

76.—(1) On the application of—
  (a) the local authority specified in a management control order ("the local authority"); or
  (b) the person who, immediately before the order was made, was the landlord of the relevant house to which the order relates ("the landlord"),
the sheriff may, if satisfied that subsection (2) or (3) applies, revoke the management control order.

(2) This subsection applies if—
  (a) the local authority; or
  (b) the landlord,
has taken the action specified in the antisocial behaviour notice.

(3) This subsection applies if, having regard to all the circumstances relating to the relevant house, it would be unreasonable for the order to continue to have effect.

DEFINITIONS
"antisocial behaviour notice": s.68(1)
"landlord": s.81(1)

"management control order":   s.74(3)
"relevant house":   s.81(1)

GENERAL NOTE
Either the landlord or the local authority can apply to the sheriff to have a management control order revoked. The grounds for ordering revocation are either that the steps specified in the original antisocial behaviour notice have been taken, though this need not have been done by the person making the application, or that continuing the order would be unreasonable.

Management control order: notification of revocation
77.—(1) Subsection (2) applies where a management control order is revoked under section 76(1) on the application of the local authority specified in the order.
(2) As soon as practicable after the order is revoked, the local authority shall—
    (a) inform—
        (i) the person who, immediately before the management control order was made, was the landlord of the house to which the order related; and
        (ii) if the authority is aware of the name and address of a person occupying the house by virtue of a tenancy or occupancy arrangement, that person,
of the revocation of the order; and
    (b) if the authority is aware of the name and address of a person who acts for the person mentioned in paragraph (a)(i) as respects a tenancy or occupancy arrangement in respect of the house, give a copy of the order to that person.
(3) If it is impracticable for the local authority to comply with the requirement in subsection (2)(a)(i), the authority need not do so.
(4) Subsection (5) applies where a management control order is revoked under section 76(1) on the application of the person who, immediately before the order was made, was the landlord of the house to which the order related.
(5) As soon as practicable after the order is revoked, the person shall—
    (a) inform the local authority specified in the order; and
    (b) any person occupying the house by virtue of a tenancy or occupancy arrangement, of the revocation of the order.

DEFINITIONS
"landlord":   s.81(1)
"management control order":   s.74(3)
"occupancy arrangement":   s.81(1)

GENERAL NOTE
Notification requirements on revocation are set out here.

Failure to comply with notice: action by authority at landlord's expense
78.—(1) Subsections (2) and (3) apply where—
    (a) a local authority serves an antisocial behaviour notice on a landlord under section 68(1);
    (b) the landlord fails to take the action specified in the notice within the time so specified; and
    (c) in consequence of that failure, it appears to the authority that it is necessary for it to take steps to deal with the antisocial behaviour described in the notice.

(2) The local authority may take such steps as it considers necessary to deal with the antisocial behaviour described in the notice.

(3) In such circumstances as the Scottish Ministers may by regulations prescribe, the landlord shall be liable for expenditure—

(a) incurred, by virtue of subsection (2), by the local authority; and

(b) of such description as may be so prescribed.

(4) Regulations under subsection (3) may include provision for or in connection with—

(a) imposing requirements on local authorities and landlords as respects arrangements for the notification and collection of expenditure of a description prescribed in the regulations;

(b) specifying arrangements for the settling of disputes arising by virtue of subsection (3).

DEFINITIONS
"antisocial behaviour notice":   s.68(1)
"landlord":   s.81(1)

GENERAL NOTE
The Scottish Ministers may prescribe what expenses incurred by a local authority in taking steps to address the antisocial behaviour described in an antisocial behaviour notice can be recovered from the landlord.

Failure to comply with notice: offence

79.—(1) Where—

(a) a local authority serves an antisocial behaviour notice on a landlord under section 68(1); and

(b) the landlord fails to take the action specified in the notice within the time so specified,

the landlord shall be guilty of an offence.

(2) A landlord guilty of an offence under this section shall be liable on summary conviction to a fine not exceeding level 5 on the standard scale.

(3) It shall be a defence for a landlord charged with an offence under subsection (1) to show that there was a reasonable excuse for the failure in question.

DEFINITIONS
"antisocial behaviour notice":   s.68(1)
"landlord":   s.81(1)

GENERAL NOTE
As well as opening up the remedies set out in ss.71 and 74, a failure to comply with an antisocial behaviour notice without reasonable excuse is an offence.

Regulations

Regulations about advice and assistance: Part 7

80. For the purposes of this Part, the Scottish Ministers may by regulations make provision requiring local authorities to provide advice and assistance of such description as may be specified in the regulations to persons of such description as may be so specified.

Interpretation

Interpretation of Part 7

81.—(1) In this Part—

"landlord", in relation to an occupancy arrangement, means the person who under the arrangement permits another to occupy the building or, as the case may be, the part of the building;

"occupancy arrangement" means any arrangement under which a person having the lawful right to occupy a building or part of a building permits another, by way of contract or otherwise, to occupy the building or, as the case may be, the part of it; but does not include a lease;

"relevant house" means, subject to subsection (2), any building or part of a building which—

    (a) is occupied as a dwelling under—

        (i) a tenancy; or

        (ii) an occupancy arrangement; and

    (b) does not fall within subsection (3).

(2) If—

(a) the same person is the landlord in relation to two or more relevant houses; and

(b) those relevant houses share the same toilet, washing or cooking facilities,

then those relevant houses shall be deemed to be a single relevant house.

(3) A building or part of a building falls within this subsection if—

(a) it is owned by—

    (i) a local authority;

    (ii) a registered social landlord; or

    (iii) Scottish Homes;

(b) it is used for the provision of—

    (i) a care home service (as defined in subsection (3) of section 2 of the Regulation of Care (Scotland) Act 2001 (asp 8));

    (ii) a school care accommodation service (as defined in subsection (4) of that section);

    (iii) an independent health care service (as defined in subsection (5) of that section); or

    (iv) a secure accommodation service (as defined in subsection (9) of that section);

(c) the house is used by a religious order the principal occupation of which is prayer, contemplation, education or the relief of suffering; or

(d) a control order under section 178 of the Housing (Scotland) Act 1987 (c.26) is in force in respect of the house.

(4) For the purposes of this Part, a person engages in antisocial behaviour if the person—

(a) acts in a manner that causes or is likely to cause alarm, distress, nuisance or annoyance; or

(b) pursues a course of conduct that causes or is likely to cause alarm, distress, nuisance or annoyance,

to a person residing in, visiting or otherwise engaging in lawful activity at, or in the locality of, a relevant house.

GENERAL NOTE

The broad scope of these definitions should be noted. The definitions cover a wide variety of premises, including hostel style accommodation and bed and breakfast accommodation, and a wide variety of arrangements under which these premises are occupied aside from those which fulfil the requirements for a tenancy under Scots law. The definitions are arguably wide enough to permit action to be taken against a parent in respect of the actions of a child. The child, after all, is permitted by the person having the lawful right to occupy the building (*i.e.* the parent/owner) to occupy the building otherwise than under a contract. Unlike the provisions in Pt.8 requiring registration of premises occupied under a lease or occupancy arrangement, there is no exclusion from the provisions of this part for leases or other arrangements involving members of the 'landlord's' family (see s.83(8)).

PART 8

HOUSING: REGISTRATION OF CERTAIN LANDLORDS

GENERAL NOTE

This part was amended substantially at Stage 2. Originally the Bill had proposed that the requirement to register would only apply in certain specified areas where there were problems of antisocial behaviour. This was extended, however, to a requirement on all landlords to register and at the same time they were made subject to certain minimum requirements. There was some resistance to this extension on the grounds that the whole issue of registration of landlords and standards for rented accommodation should be considered in a housing bill due before the Scottish Parliament in 2005. Indeed, the view of the Scottish Executive's Housing Improvement Task Force had been that a comprehensive scheme for licensing landlords should not be developed, at least in part because of the significant resource implications for local authorities. The registration required by this part is on top of any registration required where a house is in multiple occupancy and must be registered under the Civic Government (Scotland) Act 1982.

The Housing (Scotland) Bill 2005 as originally published adds to this part of the Act a Letting Code (in a new s.92A). This will be a code of practice on standards of management of those involved in letting in the private sector. The Bill also amends the factors to be taken into account in deciding if a person is a fit and proper person to act as a landlord.

Registration

Registers

82.—(1) Each local authority shall prepare and maintain a register for the purposes of this Part.

(2) Each local authority shall make its register available for public inspection at all reasonable times.

GENERAL NOTE

Local authorities must keep a public register of properties occupied under a lease or other form of occupancy arrangement and of the owners of those properties.

Application for registration

83.—(1) An application by a relevant person to a local authority for entry in the register maintained by it under section 82(1) shall specify—
  (a) the name and address of the relevant person;
  (b) the address of each house (if any) within the area of the authority which the relevant person owns and which is subject to—
      (i) a lease; or
      (ii) an occupancy arrangement,
by virtue of which an unconnected person may use the house as a dwelling;
  (c) if the relevant person has a person who acts for the person in relation to the lease or occupancy arrangement to which any house specified under paragraph (b) is subject, the name and address of the person; and
  (d) such other information as the Scottish Ministers may by regulations prescribe.

(2) Subject to subsection (3), the application shall be accompanied by such fee as the local authority may determine.

(3) The Scottish Ministers may by regulations prescribe for the purposes of subsection (2)—
(a) fees;
(b) how fees are to be arrived at;
(c) cases in which no fee shall be payable.
(4) A person who, in an application under this section—
(a) specifies information which the person knows is false in a material particular; or
(b) knowingly fails to specify information required by subsection (1), shall be guilty of an offence.
(5) A person guilty of an offence under subsection (4) shall be liable on summary conviction to a fine not exceeding level 3 on the standard scale.
(6) For the purposes of subsection (1)(b), the use of a house as a dwelling shall be disregarded if—
(a) the house is being used for the provision of—
   (i) a care home service (as defined in subsection (3) of section 2 of the Regulation of Care (Scotland) Act 2001 (asp 8));
   (ii) a school care accommodation service (as defined in subsection (4) of that section);
   (iii) an independent health care service (as defined in subsection (5) of that section); or
   (iv) a secure accommodation service (as defined in subsection (9) of that section);
(b) the house is being used by a religious order the principal occupation of which is prayer, contemplation, education or the relief of suffering;
(c) a control order under section 178 of the Housing (Scotland) Act 1987 (c.26) is in force in respect of the house; or
(d) the house is being used for holiday purposes.
(7) The Scottish Ministers may by order modify subsection (6).
(8) In this Part—
"relevant person" means a person who is not—
   (a) a local authority;
   (b) a registered social landlord; or
   (c) Scottish Homes; and
"unconnected person", in relation to a relevant person, means a person who is not a member of the family of the relevant person.

DEFINITIONS

"house":	s.101(1)
"occupancy arrangement":	s.101(1)
"relevant person":	subs.(8)
"unconnected person":	subs.(8)

GENERAL NOTE

The owner of any house which is occupied by someone who is not a member of their family under a lease or other occupancy arrangement (broadly defined in s.101(1)) (the 'relevant person') must apply to be entered in the register kept by virtue of s.82. The application must identify the relevant person, any house affected, details of anyone acting for the relevant person in relation to the lease/occupancy arrangement, and any other information required in regulations still to be made. Certain types of property are excluded under subs.(6). Aside from holiday homes and religious accommodation these are all types of accommodation subject to other controls or where the landlord is a public sector landlord (subs.(8)). During the Stage 3 debate it was indicated that subs.(7) would be used to make regulations excluding resident landlords from the requirement to register (Official Report, June 17, 2004, cols 9285–9286). It is an offence to give false information or to omit any of the information required under subs.(1) (subs.(4)).

Registration

84.—(1) This section applies where a relevant person makes an application to a local authority in accordance with section 83.

(2) Where, having considered the application—

(a) the local authority is satisfied that subsection (3) or (4) applies, the authority shall enter the relevant person in the register maintained by the authority under section 82(1);

(b) the authority is not satisfied that either of those subsections applies, the authority shall refuse to enter the relevant person in the register.

(3) This subsection applies where—

(a) under paragraph (b) of section 83(1), the application—

(i) does not specify a house; or

(ii) specifies a house (or two or more houses);

(b) under paragraph (c) of that section, the application does not specify the name and address of a person; and

(c) the relevant person is a fit and proper person to act as landlord under—

(i) a lease; or

(ii) an occupancy arrangement,

by virtue of which an unconnected person may use a house as a dwelling.

(4) This subsection applies where—

(a) under paragraph (b) of section 83(1), the application specifies at least one house;

(b) under paragraph (c) of that section, the application specifies the name and address of a person;

(c) subsection (3)(c) applies; and

(d) the person is a fit and proper person to act for a landlord such as is mentioned in that subsection in relation to the lease or, as the case may be, arrangement.

(5) An entry in a register under subsection (2)(a) shall state, in relation to the relevant person, the information specified by virtue of paragraphs (a) to (c) of section 83(1) in the application made by the relevant person.

(6) Subject to sections 88(8) and 89(1), where a local authority makes an entry in a register under subsection (2)(a), the authority shall remove the entry from the register on the expiry of the period of 3 years beginning with the day on which the entry is made.

DEFINITIONS
"fit and proper person":   see s.85
"house":   s.101(1)
"relevant person":   s.83(8)

GENERAL NOTE

The local authority can grant an application to register made under s.83 in two circumstances. The first of these applies where there is no-one acting on behalf of the applicant in connection with the (existing or proposed) lease or other occupancy rights affecting the property. Here the authority must be satisfied that the applicant is a fit and proper person to act as landlord under the lease or other arrangement. Registration can then take place whether or not the applicant identifies a property to be let or otherwise occupied. This provision (in subs.(3)(a)(i)) allows an applicant to obtain clearance as a fit and proper person before investing in a property to let, if a property is then purchased for occupation by a third party an application to amend the register can be made under s.88.

The second circumstance applies where the owner has appointed someone to act on their behalf in relation to the lease or other occupancy right. Here at least one house must be specified in the application and the authority must be satisfied that both the owner and the person acting on their behalf are fit and proper persons.

Entries made in the register last for three years unless grounds arise within that time for removal from the register. A fresh application for registration will therefore be required as the three year period draws to an end. If registration is refused there is a right of appeal under s.92.

Section 84: considerations

85.—(1) In deciding for the purposes of section 84(3) or (4) whether the relevant person or, as the case may be, the person is a fit and proper person, the local authority shall have regard (among other things) to any material falling within subsections (2) to (4).

(2) Material falls within this subsection if it shows that the relevant person or, as the case may be, the person has—

(a) committed any offence involving—
    (i) fraud or other dishonesty;
    (ii) violence; or
    (iii) drugs;
(b) practised unlawful discrimination on grounds of sex, colour, race, ethnic or national origins or disability in, or in connection with, the carrying on of any business; or
(c) contravened any provision of—
    (i) the law relating to housing; or
    (ii) landlord and tenant law.

(3) Material falls within this subsection if it relates to any actings of the relevant person or, as the case may be, the person as respects antisocial behaviour affecting a house—

(a) subject to a lease or occupancy arrangement such as is mentioned in section 84(3)(c); and
(b) in relation to which the relevant person was (or is) the landlord under the lease or arrangement or, as the case may be, the person was (or is) acting for the landlord in relation to the lease or arrangement.

(4) Material falls within this subsection if it appears to the authority that the material is relevant to the question of whether the relevant person or, as the case may be, the person is a fit and proper person.

(5) In subsection (3), "actings" includes failure to act.

DEFINITIONS
"antisocial behaviour":   s.101
"relevant person":   s.83(8)

GENERAL NOTE
   In deciding whether a person is a fit and proper person the authority has to consider three sorts of material:

(a) Material indicating a contravention of the law. This can either be a criminal offence involving violence, dishonesty or drugs, unlawful discrimination or a contravention of housing or landlord and tenant law. An example of the last might be unlawful eviction. Note that neither a previous conviction nor any of the other sorts of behaviour listed in subs.(2) are in themselves an automatic bar to being considered to be a fit and proper person.
(b) Any acts or omissions respect of antisocial behaviour in any house let or subject to an occupancy arrangement. The acts and omissions are those of the owner of the property affected and any person acting on their behalf. Essentially this is looking at steps taken by the landlord to tackle past antisocial behaviour.

Any other relevant material, this could be both negative and positive, *e.g.* evidence of a long period of good behaviour after a conviction for a violent offence.
   This section is prospectively amended by the Housing (Scotland) Bill 2005. One of the amendments is to incorporate contravention of the Letting Code provided for in the Bill as a

relevant consideration under subs.(2)(c). Another is to include as relevant material any agreement between the relevant person (see General Note to s.83) and someone acting on their behalf as regards occupancy arrangements for a dwelling.

Notification of registration or refusal to register

86.—(1) Where a local authority—
  (a) enters a person in its register under paragraph (a) of section 84(2); or
  (b) refuses to enter a person in its register under paragraph (b) of that section,
     the authority shall, as soon as practicable after doing so, give notice of the fact to the person.

(2) Where a local authority refuses to enter a person in its register under section 84(2)(b), the authority shall, as soon as practicable after doing so, send notice of the fact to—
  (a) each address specified by virtue of paragraph (b) of section 83(1) in the application for registration; and
  (b) if, by virtue of paragraph (c) of section 83(1), the application specified the name and address of a person, that person.

GENERAL NOTE
    A decision to register or refuse registration must be notified to the applicant and anyone acting on their behalf. In addition, notification must be sent to all the houses which are owned by the applicant and let out or subject to an occupancy arrangement. This will ensure that 'tenants' (in a broad sense) will be notified of the decision of the authority and in particular of any refusal to register.

Duty of registered person to provide information to local authority

87.—(1) This section applies where a person is registered by a local authority.

(2) If in consequence of a change in circumstances any information provided by the person to the local authority by virtue of section 83(1) or, as the case may be, this subsection, becomes inaccurate, the person shall, as soon as practicable after the inaccuracy arises, give notice in writing to the authority of the change that has occurred.

(3) Subject to subsection (4), any notice given under subsection (2) shall be accompanied by such fee as the local authority may determine.

(4) The Scottish Ministers may by regulations prescribe for the purposes of subsection (3)—
  (a) fees;
  (b) how fees are to be arrived at;
  (c) cases in which no fee shall be payable.

(5) A person who, without reasonable excuse, fails to comply with subsection (2) shall be guilty of an offence.

(6) A person guilty of an offence under subsection (5) shall be liable on summary conviction to a fine not exceeding level 3 on the standard scale.

GENERAL NOTE
    If there are any changes in respect of the information provided in the application for registration or in any later notification under this section this must be notified to the authority. An example would be the acquisition of a further property to let. Failure to do this without reasonable excuse is an offence.

Registered person: appointment of agent

88.—(1) Subsection (2) applies where—
  (a) a person is registered by a local authority (the "registered person"); and

(b) the registered person appoints a person to act for the person in relation to—
   (i) a lease; or
   (ii) occupancy arrangement,
by virtue of which an unconnected person may use as a dwelling a house within the area of the authority which the registered person owns.

(2) The registered person shall, as soon as practicable after appointing the person, give notice in writing to the local authority of the appointment.

(3) The local authority shall, as soon as practicable after being given notice under subsection (2), determine whether the condition in subsection (4) is satisfied in relation to the person appointed.

(4) The condition is that the person is a fit and proper person to act for the registered person in relation to a lease or occupancy arrangement such as is mentioned in subsection (1)(b).

(5) Subsections (2) to (5) of section 85 shall apply for the purposes of subsection (4) as those subsections apply for the purposes of subsection (1) of that section.

(6) If the local authority determines that the condition in subsection (4) is satisfied—
(a) the registered person shall be deemed, with effect from the date of the determination, to be registered by virtue of subsection (4) of section 84; and
(b) the local authority shall give the registered person notice in writing of that fact.

(7) Subsection (6)(a) shall not affect the calculation of the period mentioned in section 84(6).

(8) If the local authority determines that the condition in subsection (4) is not satisfied, the authority shall remove the registered person from the register.

DEFINITIONS
"fit and proper person":   see s.85
"registered person":   subs.(1)(a)

GENERAL NOTE
A person who is registered in the register may decide to appoint someone to act on their behalf in respect of the let or other occupancy rights granted in respect of property, for example a letting or management agent. If that is done the local authority must be notified. The authority then has to decide whether the person appointed is a fit and proper person taking account of the materials set out in s.85. Where it is decided that the person does fall into this category the registration will be confirmed and the ground of registration will change from s.84(3)—s.84(4) (subs.(6)). However, if the person who is appointed is not a fit and proper person the result will be that the registration will essentially be withdrawn and the person who was formerly registered will be removed from the register subject to a right of appeal under s.92.

Removal from register
89.—(1) Where—
(a) a person is registered by a local authority; and
(b) subsection (2) or (3) applies,
   the authority shall remove the person from its register.
(2) This subsection applies where—
(a) the person was registered by virtue of section 84(3); and
(b) paragraph (c) of that section no longer applies.
(3) This subsection applies where—
(a) the person was registered by virtue of section 84(4); and

(b) paragraph (c) or (d) of that section no longer applies.

GENERAL NOTE
A local authority can remove an owner from the register either if he/she is no longer a fit and proper person or if the person they have appointed to act on their behalf in relation to the lease or occupancy right is no longer a fit and proper person. There is a right of appeal under s.92.

Notification of removal from register: registered person
   90.—(1) Subsection (2) applies where under section 88(8) or 89(1) a local authority removes a person from the register maintained by it under section 82(1).
   (2) As soon as practicable after the removal, the local authority shall give the person notice in writing of—
   (a) the removal; and
   (b) the date of the removal.
   (3) Notice under subsection (2) shall be given to the person at the address which, immediately before the removal, was specified as being the address of the person in the entry for the person in the register.
   (4) For the purposes of subsection (2), notice is given by being sent by the recorded delivery service.

GENERAL NOTE
Notification of a removal from the register must be made to the person registered (*i.e.* the owner of the house) by recorded delivery. Additional notification is required under s.91.

Notification of removal from register: other persons
   91.—(1) Subsection (2) applies where under section 88(8) or 89(1) a local authority removes a person from the register maintained by it under section 82(1).
   (2) As soon as practicable after the removal, the local authority shall give notice of the removal and the date of the removal to—
   (a) the address of each house that, immediately before the removal, was entered in the person's entry in the register; and
   (b) if the authority is aware of the name and address of a person who acts for the person whose name was removed from the register in relation to a lease or occupancy arrangement such as is mentioned in section 88(1)(b), that person.

GENERAL NOTE
As well as notifying the person registered of removal from the register the local authority must also notify anyone acting on behalf of that person and send notification to any house entered in the person's entry in the register. This last will ensure notification to tenants and others occupying such houses.

Appeal against refusal to register or removal from register
   92.—(1) Subsection (2) applies where—
   (a) under section 84(2)(b) a local authority refuses to enter a person in the register maintained by it under section 82(1); or
   (b) under section 88(8) or 89(1) an authority removes a person from the register.
   (2) The sheriff may, on the application of the person, make an order—
   (a) requiring the authority to enter the person in the register; and
   (b) specifying whether the entry shall be deemed to be made by virtue of subsection (3) or (4) of section 84.

(3) Where by virtue of subsection (2) a local authority enters a person in the register maintained by it under section 82(1), the entry shall be deemed to have been made under subsection (2)(a) of section 84 by virtue of the subsection specified in the order.

(4) An application such as is mentioned in subsection (2) shall be made by summary application.

(5) An appeal against the decision of a sheriff granting or refusing an application under subsection (2) shall be made to the sheriff principal and shall be made within the period of 21 days beginning with the day on which the decision appealed against was made.

(6) The decision of the sheriff principal on an appeal under this section shall be final.

GENERAL NOTE

A decision to refuse registration or to remove from the register can be appealed to the sheriff. There is a further appeal to the sheriff principal, but no further.

Enforcement

Offences

93.—(1) Where—
  (a) a relevant person owns a house within the area of a local authority which is subject to—
      (i) a lease; or
      (ii) an occupancy arrangement,
by virtue of which an unconnected person may use the house as a dwelling; and
  (b) the relevant person is not registered by that authority,
      the relevant person shall be guilty of an offence.

(2) Where—
  (a) a relevant person is not registered by a local authority; and
  (b) in relation to a house that the relevant person owns in the area of the authority, the relevant person communicates with another person with a view to entering into a lease or an occupancy arrangement such as is mentioned in subsection (1)(a),
      the relevant person shall be guilty of an offence.

(3) Where subsection (5) applies, nothing in subsection (1) makes it an offence for a relevant person to own a house which is subject to a lease or, as the case may be, occupancy arrangement such as is mentioned in subsection (1).

(4) Where subsection (5) applies, nothing in subsection (2) makes it an offence for a relevant person to communicate with another person with a view to entering into a lease or, as the case may be, occupancy arrangement such as is mentioned in subsection (2).

(5) This subsection applies where—
  (a) the relevant person has made an application under section 83 to the local authority within whose area the house is situated; but
  (b) the application has not been determined under section 84 by the authority.

(6) It shall be a defence for a person charged with an offence under subsection (1) or (2) to show that there was a reasonable excuse for acting in the way charged.

(7) A person guilty of an offence under subsection (1) or (2) shall be liable on summary conviction to a fine not exceeding level 5 on the standard scale.

GENERAL NOTE
    One of the enforcement mechanisms for the register is that it is a offence for an unregistered person to let out a house, enter into an occupancy arrangement in respect of it or communicate with anyone with a view to entering such a ease or arrangement. There is an exception where an application for registration has been made but not determined. It is defence that there was a reasonable excuse for acting in the way which would otherwise amount to an offence.

Circumstances in which no rent to be payable

94.—(1) Where a local authority is satisfied that the conditions in subsection (2) are met in relation to a house within its area, the authority may serve a notice under this section on the persons mentioned in subsection (5).
    (2) Those conditions are—
    (a) that the owner of the house is a relevant person;
    (b) that the house is subject to—
        (i) a lease; or
        (ii) an occupancy arrangement,
            by virtue of which an unconnected person may use the house as a dwelling;
    (c) that the relevant person is not registered by the local authority; and
    (d) that, having regard to all the circumstances relating to the relevant person, it is appropriate for a notice to be served under this section.
    (3) Where a notice is served under this section, during the relevant period—
    (a) no rent shall be payable under any lease or occupancy arrangement in respect of the house to which the notice relates;
    (b) no other consideration shall be payable or exigible under any such lease or occupancy arrangement.
    (4) A notice served under this section shall specify—
    (a) the name of the relevant person to whom it relates;
    (b) the address of the house to which it relates;
    (c) the effect of subsection (3); and
    (d) the date on which it takes effect (which must not be earlier than the day after the day on which it is served).
    (5) Those persons are—
    (a) the relevant person;
    (b) if the local authority is aware of the name and address of a person who has, by virtue of a lease or an occupancy arrangement such as is mentioned in subsection (2)(b), the use of the house to which the notice relates, that person; and
    (c) if the local authority is aware of the name and address of a person who acts for the relevant person in relation to such a lease or an occupancy arrangement, that person.
    (6) If—
    (a) the local authority is unable to identify the relevant person, it may serve the notice under this section by publishing it in two or more newspapers (of which one shall, if practicable, be a local newspaper) circulating in the locality of the house to which the notice relates;
    (b) the local authority is aware of the relevant person's identity but is unable to ascertain the relevant person's current address, it may serve the notice under this section by serving it on the landlord—

(i) at the house to which the notice relates; and

(ii) if it is aware of a previous address of the relevant person, at that address.

(7) The condition mentioned in subsection (2)(c) shall not be taken to be met where—

(a) the relevant person has made an application under section 83 to the local authority in whose area the house is situated; but

(b) the application has not been determined under section 84 by the authority.

(8) Except as provided in subsection (3), nothing in this Part affects the validity of any lease or occupancy arrangement under which an unconnected person has the use as a dwelling of a house during the relevant period.

(9) Where a local authority is aware of the name and address of a person mentioned in paragraph (b) or, as the case may be, (c) of subsection (5), failure to serve a notice on the person shall not affect the validity of the notice.

(10) In this section, "relevant period" means the period beginning with the date specified in the notice and ending with the earlier of—

(a) the revocation of the notice under section 95(2); or

(b) where the effect of the decision made on an appeal under section 97 is that rent or, as the case may be, other consideration is payable or exigible, that decision.

DEFINITIONS

"occupancy arrangement":	s.101(1)
"relevant period":	subs.(10)
"relevant person":	s.83(8)
"unconnected person":	s.83(8)

GENERAL NOTE

In addition to the criminal penalties for unregistered landlord there is also a civil penalty, provided by this section. The penalty involves the suspension of payment, whether in the form of rent or other payment, for the occupation of a house. Suspension follows service of a notice by the local authority. The power to serve the notice arises where the owner of the house let or subject to an occupancy arrangement is not registered in the register kept under s.82 while required to be registered by s.83 and it is appropriate to serve a notice. The content of the notice and the service requirements are set out in subss (4)—(6) and (9). The notice will remain in effect until either revoked under s.95 or successfully appealed under s.97.

Service of the notice does not affect any rights to occupy (subs.(8)). No notice can be served where an application as been made for registration but not yet determined by the local authority (subs.(7)). There is a right of appeal against service of an order (s.97).

Notices under section 94: revocation

95.—(1) Subsection (2) applies where a local authority serves a notice under section 94 in relation to a house.

(2) If (whether on the application of a person having an interest in the case or otherwise) the local authority which served the notice is satisfied that the conditions mentioned in section 94(2) are no longer met in relation to the house, the authority shall, with effect from such day as it may specify, revoke the notice.

(3) The revocation of a notice under subsection (2) shall not operate so as to make a person liable to pay any rent or other consideration in respect of the period during which the notice was in force.

GENERAL NOTE

If the local authority is satisfied that the grounds for making an order suspending payment of rent set out in s.94(2) no longer exist it must revoke the order. This might happen, for example, if the owner of the house affected successfully applies for registration (though, presumably, the contravention of housing law involved in unregistered letting would be a factor to be considered under s.84 in deciding if the/she was a fit and proper person). Revocation of the order does not make the occupier/tenant liable to pay back rent due during the period when the order was in force. Refusal of a local authority to revoke an order following application by someone with an interest in the case can be appealed (s.97).

Notification of revocation of notice

96.—(1) Subsection (2) applies where a local authority revokes a notice under section 95 in relation to a house.

(2) As soon as practicable after revoking the notice, the local authority shall give notice of the fact to—

(a) the relevant person;

(b) if the local authority is aware of the name and address of a person who has, by virtue of a lease or an occupancy arrangement such as is mentioned in section 94(2)(b), the use of the house to which the notice relates, that person; and

(c) if the local authority is aware of the name and address of a person who acts for the relevant person in relation to such a lease or an occupancy arrangement, that person.

(3) Where a local authority is aware of the name and address of a person mentioned in paragraph (b) or, as the case may be, (c) of subsection (2), failure to serve a notice on the person may not be founded on in any proceedings.

DEFINITIONS
"house": s.101(1)
"occupancy arrangement": s.101(1)
"relevant person": s.83(8)

Appeals

97.—(1) A relevant person on whom a notice under section 94 is served may, before the expiry of the period of 21 days beginning with the date specified by virtue of subsection (4)(d) of that section in the notice, appeal to the sheriff against the decision of the local authority to serve the notice.

(2) Where, on the application of a person having an interest, a local authority makes a decision refusing to revoke a notice under section 95(2), the person may, before the expiry of the period of 21 days beginning with the day on which the decision is made, appeal to the sheriff against the decision.

(3) Subsection (4) applies where a person appeals against a decision such as is mentioned in subsection (1) or (2).

(4) The person shall (in addition to complying with any other requirements as to notification imposed by virtue of any enactment) give notice to the person who has the use as a dwelling of the house to which the notice relates (the "tenant") of such matters as may be prescribed by the Scottish Ministers by regulations.

(5) Regulations under subsection (4) may include provision for or in connection with—

(a) the form of the notice;

(b) the manner and timing of service of the notice.

(6) If a person fails to comply with subsection (4), the court hearing the appeal may not require the tenant to pay any sums that, but for the making of the order, would have been due by the tenant.

(7) The Scottish Ministers may by regulations make provision for or in connection with specifying other circumstances in which the sheriff princi-

pal shall not require a tenant to pay any sums that, but for the making of the order, would have been due by the tenant.

(8) Regulations under subsection (7) may in particular include provision—

(a) specifying procedures;

(b) imposing obligations on landlords.

DEFINITIONS

"relevant person":   s.83(8)

"tenant":   subs.(4)

GENERAL NOTE

There is a right of appeal to the sheriff against both service of a notice under 94 and refusal of an application to revoke such a notice. Where an appeal is made under this section the person occupying the house affected must be notified of the appeal. If notification is not made then the sheriff cannot order the occupier to pay back rent for the period between service of the notice and the successful appeal. Further restrictions on the ability of the sheriff to order payment of back rent can be made by regulation, see the General Note to s.72.

Grants

Grants to local authorities

98.—(1) The Scottish Ministers may make a grant to a local authority in respect of costs incurred by the authority by virtue of this Part.

(2) The payment of a grant under subsection (1) may be made subject to such conditions (including conditions as to repayment) as the Scottish Ministers may determine.

GENERAL NOTE

Considerable concerns have been expressed about the cost implications for local authorities of creating and maintaining a register. This section provides for grant assistance to be given to local authorities.

Regulations

Regulations about advice and assistance: Part 8

99. For the purposes of this Part, the Scottish Ministers may by regulations make provision requiring local authorities to provide advice and assistance of such description as may be specified in the regulations to persons of such description as may be so specified.

Amendment of Housing (Scotland) Act 1988

Amendment of Housing (Scotland) Act 1988

100. In subsection (6)(a) of section 18 of the Housing (Scotland) Act 1988 (c.43) (orders for possession)—

(a) the word "or", where it thirdly occurs, shall be repealed; and

(b) after "10" there shall be inserted ", Ground 15".

GENERAL NOTE

The effect of this section is to add an additional ground on the basis of which a sheriff can grant an order for possession during a contractual assured tenancy. The ground added is that concerned with conviction for using the house for immoral or illegal purposes, conviction for an imprisonable offence in the vicinity of the house and antisocial behaviour. Before this can operate, however, the terms of the contractual tenancy must make provision for the tenancy to be terminated on that ground (Housing (Scotland) Act 1988 (c.43), s.18(6)(b)).

Interpretation

Interpretation of Part 8

101.—(1) In this Part—

"house" means, subject to subsection (2), a building or part of a building occupied or intended to be occupied as a dwelling;

"landlord", in relation to an occupancy arrangement, means the person who under the arrangement permits another to occupy the building or, as the case may be, the part of the building;

"occupancy arrangement" means any arrangement under which a person having the lawful right to occupy a house permits another, by way of contract or otherwise, to occupy the house or, as the case may be, part of it; but does not include a lease;

"registered", in relation to a relevant person and a local authority, means entered by virtue of section 84(2)(a) in the register maintained by the authority under section 82(1); and cognate expressions shall be construed accordingly;

"relevant person" has the meaning given by section 83(8);

"unconnected person" has the meaning given by section 83(8); and

"use as a dwelling" shall be construed in accordance with section 83(6).

(2) If two or more dwellings within a building share the same toilet, washing or cooking facilities, then those dwellings shall be deemed to be a single house for the purposes of this Part.

(3) For the purposes of this Part, any reference to a person's being a member of another's family shall be construed in accordance with section 108(1) and (2) of the Housing (Scotland) Act 2001 (asp 10).

(4) For the purposes of this Part, a person engages in antisocial behaviour if the person—

(a) acts in a manner that causes or is likely to cause alarm, distress, nuisance or annoyance; or

(b) pursues a course of conduct that causes or is likely to cause alarm, distress, nuisance or annoyance,

to a person residing in, visiting or otherwise engaging in lawful activity at, or in the locality of, a house; and "antisocial behaviour" shall be construed accordingly.

PART 9

PARENTING ORDERS

GENERAL NOTE

This part of the Act makes provision for parenting orders, which impose certain conditions on the parents of children. The grounds for making an order are set out in s.102, with additional procedural rules contained in s.108, and issues to be considered by the sheriff set out in ss.109 and 110. Once made the order can be reviewed by the sheriff (s.105), and failure to comply with an order is a criminal offence (s.107).

Parenting Orders have been in place in England and Wales since 2000, with the scope of these being extended in 2003 (the main provisions are the Crime and Disorder Act 1998, ss.8–10 and the Antisocial Behaviour Act 2003 (c.38), ss.25–29). Research evidence from England on the relationship between poor parenting and offending amongst children (Graham and Bowling, *Young People and Crime*, Home Office Research Study 145, 1995) and on the effectiveness of parenting programmes, in part carried out under parenting orders (Ghate and Ramella, *Positive Parenting: The Effectiveness of the Youth Justice Board's Parenting Programme*, Youth Justice Board, 2002), were both cited in support of the introduction of these orders into Scotland (see *Putting Our Communities First*, pp.35–36).

A national pilot of parenting orders started on commencement of this part of the Act and is scheduled to last for 3 years. *Guidance on Parenting Orders* was issued in April 2005 and is available at: http://www.scotland.gov.uk/Resource/Doc/37432/0011355.pdf

Applications
102.—(1) The court may make a parenting order in respect of a parent of a child where—
(a) subsection (2) or (3) applies; and
(b) the Scottish Ministers have notified the court that the local authority for the area in which the parent ordinarily resides has made arrangements that would enable the order to be complied with.
(2) This subsection applies where—
(a) the application for the order is made by the appropriate local authority; and
(b) the court is satisfied that—
   (i) the behaviour condition; or
   (ii) the conduct condition,
is met.
(3) This subsection applies where—
(a) the application for the order is made by the Principal Reporter; and
(b) the court is satisfied that—
   (i) the behaviour condition;
   (ii) the conduct condition; or
   (iii) the welfare condition,
is met.
(4) The behaviour condition is—
(a) that the child has engaged in antisocial behaviour; and
(b) that the making of the order is desirable in the interests of preventing the child from engaging in further such behaviour.
(5) The conduct condition is—
(a) that the child has engaged in criminal conduct; and
(b) that the making of the order is desirable in the interests of preventing the child from engaging in further such conduct.
(6) The welfare condition is that the making of the order is desirable in the interests of improving the welfare of the child.
(7) For the purposes of subsection (5), a child engages in criminal conduct if the child engages in conduct that constitutes a criminal offence (or would do so if the child had attained the age of 8 years).
(8) An application under this section shall be made by summary application to the sheriff of the sheriffdom where the parent ordinarily resides.
(9) Before an application is made under this section—
(a) by a local authority, it shall consult the Principal Reporter;
(b) by the Principal Reporter, the Principal Reporter shall consult the appropriate local authority.
(10) In this section, "appropriate local authority" means the local authority for the area where the child ordinarily resides.

Definitions
"antisocial behaviour":   s.143
"appropriate local authority": subs.(10)
"behaviour condition":   subs.(4)
"conduct condition":   subs.(5)
"criminal conduct":   subs.(7)
"parent":   s.117
"parenting order":   s.103(1)
"welfare condition":   subs.(6)

General Note
Both the local authority for the area where a child lives and the Principal Reporter can

apply to the sheriff for a parenting order. In some circumstances the Reporter may be instructed by a court (s.114) or by a children's hearing (s.116) to consider whether to apply for an order and the sheriff making an antisocial behaviour order also has the power to make a parenting order (s.13). Before an application is made there must be consultation between the local authority and the Reporter (subs.(9)), and there are specific investigation and reporting duties placed on the Reporter (s.113).

An order can only be made where there are local arrangements in place to allow the order to be given effect to, otherwise the grounds for making the order depend on whether the application is made by a local authority (subs.(2)) or by the Reporter (subs.(3)). Aside from these, the considerations relevant to deciding whether or not to exercise the discretion to make an order are set out in s.109, which includes the requirement that in making an order the paramount consideration is the welfare of the child.

Subss (4) and (5)
In each of these subsections the court has to be satisfied that the child has behaved in a certain way in the past. There is no reason why the standard of proof here should differ from that required in the case of proof of past antisocial behaviour where an application is made for an antisocial behaviour order. As discussed in the General Note to s.4, this standard will be proof beyond a reasonable doubt (see also: Home Office/Youth Justice Board/Department for Constitutional Affairs, *Parenting Contracts and Orders Guidance*, February 2004, para.5.6). By virtue of subs.(7) a child under the age of eight may be found to have engaged in criminal conduct, even though they are below the age of criminal responsibility in Scotland.

As regards the behaviour ground for an order, the *Guidance* (para.39) indicates that: "Parenting orders are not intended to address behaviour that is merely different, or behaviour that is the result of a medical or developmental condition or a mental disorder and should not be used to promote the harassment of individuals or groups for behaviour that results from being of a different race or religion."

Parenting orders

Parenting orders
103.—(1) A parenting order is an order requiring the specified person—
(a) to comply, during a specified period—
    (i) beginning with the making of the order; and
    (ii) not exceeding 12 months,
       with such requirements as are specified; and
(b) subject to subsection (2), to attend, during a specified period—
    (i) falling within the specified period mentioned in paragraph (a); and
    (ii) not exceeding 3 months,
       such counselling or guidance sessions as may be directed by a supervising officer appointed by the relevant local authority.

(2) Where a parenting order has been made in respect of the person on a previous occasion in the interests of the child in whose interests the order is to be made, the order need not include a requirement under subsection (1)(b).

(3) The Scottish Ministers may by order amend the number of months mentioned in—
(a) subsection (1)(a)(ii); and
(b) subsection (1)(b)(ii).

(4) In subsection (1), "specified" means specified in the order.

GENERAL NOTE
A parenting order can last up to 12 months and will have a compulsory requirement to attend a parenting programme run by the local authority for up to three months of the duration of the order (subs.(1)(b)). The requirement to attend such a programme need not be made if a previous parenting order has been made in respect of the parent in relation to the

same child. In addition, the court can impose additional requirements, for example to attend a residential parenting programme, or to ensure that the child attends school, avoids contact with certain other children, or is effectively supervised at certain times. Any requirement imposed must avoid, as far as practicable, conflict with religious beliefs or with the demands work or education (s.110). It has been held that parenting orders are compliant with Art.8 of the European Convention on Human Rights, *R. (on the application of M) v Inner London Crown Court* [2004] 1 FCR 178. Despite this it might be argued in an individual case that the evidence was not sufficient to justify the interference with the Art.8 rights of the parent.

Matters following making of order

Notification of making of order

104.—(1) The clerk of the court by which a parenting order is made shall cause a copy of the order to be—

(a) given to the person specified in the order; or

(b) sent to the person so specified by registered post or the recorded delivery service.

(2) A certificate of posting of a letter sent under subsection (1)(b) issued by the postal operator concerned shall be sufficient evidence of the sending of the letter on the day specified in such certificate.

(3) In subsection (2), "postal operator" has the meaning given by section 125(1) of the Postal Services Act 2000 (c.26).

DEFINITIONS
"parenting order":   s.103(1)

Review of order

105.—(1) On the application of a relevant applicant the court that made a parenting order may, if it considers that it would be appropriate to do so—

(a) revoke the order; or

(b) vary the order by—

    (i) deleting any of the requirements specified in the order;

    (ii) adding a new requirement;

    (iii) altering the period specified for the purpose of section 103(1)(b).

(2) In subsection (1), "relevant applicant" means—

(a) the person specified in the order;

(b) the child in respect of whom the order was made;

(c) the local authority for the area in which the person specified in the order ordinarily resides.

(3) Before an application is made under subsection (1) by a local authority, it shall consult the Principal Reporter.

(4) Where an application under subsection (1) for the revocation or, as the case may be, variation, of a parenting order is refused, another such application by the same applicant under that subsection for revocation or, as the case may be, variation, may be made only with the consent of the court that made the order.

(5) Where the court that made a parenting order is satisfied that—

(a) the person specified in the order proposes to change, or has changed, the person's place of ordinary residence; and

(b) it is appropriate to make an order specifying the sheriff of another sheriffdom as the court that may entertain applications under subsection (1),

it may make such an order; and in such a case, this section shall be read as if references to the court that made the order were references to that sheriff.

DEFINITIONS
"parenting order": s.103(1)

GENERAL NOTE
Either the local authority, the parent subject to a parenting order or their child can apply for variation or revocation of the order. In any application the court is empowered to add or delete requirements or to alter the period of attendance at a parenting programme. Once one application for revocation or amendment has been made the same person cannot make another application without the consent of the court (subs.(4)). In deciding any application under this section the procedures and considerations set out in ss.108 and 109 apply. The decision of the court can be appealed (s.106). Finally, subs.(5) allows for transfer of the parenting order if the parent moves.

Appeals

106. An interlocutor—
(a) varying, or refusing to vary, a parenting order; or
(b) making a parenting order under section 13,
is an appealable interlocutor.

DEFINITIONS
"parenting order": s.103(1)

Failure to comply with order

107.—(1) If the person specified in a parenting order fails without reasonable excuse to comply with—
(a) any requirement specified in the order; or
(b) any direction given under the order,
the person shall be guilty of an offence.
(2) A person guilty of an offence under subsection (1) shall be liable on summary conviction to a fine not exceeding level 3 on the standard scale.
(3) In determining the sentence to be imposed on a person guilty of an offence under subsection (1) a court shall take into consideration the welfare of any child in respect of whom the person is a parent.

DEFINITIONS
"child": s.117
"parent": s.117
"parenting order": s.103(1)

GENERAL NOTE
Failure to comply with the terms of a parenting order is an offence, unless there is a reasonable excuse for the failure. In considering the appropriate sentence on conviction the court must consider the welfare of any children to whom the person convicted is parent.
The *Guidance* at paras 81 to 83 sets out the process to be followed by the responsible person (the person in the local authority nominated to oversee delivery of the order) in cases of failure to comply with requirements of the order.

General requirements

Procedural requirements

108.—(1) Before making, varying or revoking a parenting order, a court shall—
(a) having regard to the age and maturity of the child, so far as practicable—
(i) give the child an opportunity to indicate whether the child wishes to express views; and

    (ii) if the child so wishes, give the child an opportunity to express those views;

(b) give the parent the opportunity to be heard;

(c) obtain information about the family circumstances of the parent and the likely effect of the order on those circumstances.

(2) Before making a parenting order, the court shall explain in ordinary language—

(a) the effect of the order and of the requirements proposed to be included in it;

(b) the consequences of failing to comply with the order;

(c) the powers the court has under section 105; and

(d) the entitlement of the parent to appeal against the making of the order.

(3) Before varying or revoking a parenting order, the court shall explain in ordinary language the effect of the variation or, as the case may be, revocation.

(4) Subsections (2) and (3) apply only where the parent is present in court.

(5) Failure to comply with subsection (2) or (3) shall not affect the validity of the order made.

(6) Without prejudice to the generality of subsection (1)(a), a child who is at least 12 years of age shall be presumed to be of sufficient age and maturity to form a view.

DEFINITIONS

"child":	s.117
"parent":	s.117
"parenting order":	s.103(1)

GENERAL NOTE

Two procedural requirements are imposed before a parenting order or an order revoking or varying it can be made. The first requirement is that the child and the parent are to be given the opportunity to be heard and, in addition, information is to be obtained about the family circumstances of the parent and the likely effect of the order on those circumstances. This information will usually be in the form of a report from the local authority. Children's rights to be heard will depend on their age and maturity, with children aged 12 or over deemed to be able to form a view regarding the court proceedings.

The second requirement is a requirement to explain the order to the parent. This is not required where the parent is not present in court, and even where the parent is present a failure to explain will not affect the validity of the order made.

General considerations relating to making, varying and revoking order

109.—(1) Where a court is determining whether to make, vary or revoke a parenting order its paramount consideration shall be the welfare of the child.

(2) Where a court is determining whether to make a parenting order it shall have regard to—

(a) such views as the child has expressed in relation to that matter by virtue of paragraph (a) of subsection (1) of section 108;

(b) the information obtained in relation to that matter by virtue of paragraph (c) of that subsection;

(c) whether (and if so the extent to which) the parent has, at any time that appears to the court to be relevant, taken relevant voluntary steps; and

(d) any other behaviour of the parent that appears to the court to be relevant.

(3) Where a court is determining whether to vary or revoke a parenting order it shall have regard to—

(a) such views as the child has expressed in relation to that matter by virtue of paragraph (a) of subsection (1) of section 108;

(b) the information obtained in relation to that matter by virtue of paragraph (c) of that subsection; and

(c) any behaviour of the parent that appears to the court to be relevant.

(4) In subsection (2)(c), "relevant voluntary steps" means—

(a) where the court is determining whether to—

    (i) make a parenting order under section 13; or

    (ii) make a parenting order under subsection (1) of section 102 in respect of the condition mentioned in subsection (4) of that section,

voluntary steps intended to be in the interests of preventing the child from engaging in antisocial behaviour;

(b) where the court is determining whether to make a parenting order under subsection (1) of section 102 in respect of the condition mentioned in subsection (5) of that section, voluntary steps intended to be in the interests of preventing the child from engaging in criminal conduct;

(c) where the court is determining whether to make a parenting order under subsection (1) of section 102 in respect of the condition mentioned in subsection (6) of that section, voluntary steps intended to be in the interests of improving the welfare of the child.

DEFINITIONS

"child":	s.117
"parent":	s.117
"parenting order":	s.103(1)
"relevant voluntary steps":	subs.(4)

GENERAL NOTE

This section sets out the matters which the court must consider before a parenting order or an order revoking or varying it can be made. Paramount consideration must be given to the welfare of the child. In addition, consideration must be given to the views expressed by the child, the information obtained by the court on the family circumstances of the parent, and any other relevant behaviour of the parent. Perhaps strangely there seems to be no requirement to consider any views expressed by the parent in exercise of their right to be heard under s.108(1)(b). In addition, but only when considering making a parenting order, consideration must be given to any voluntary steps taken by the parent to address the behaviour or concerns underlying the application for the order (subs.(4)). Note that the fact that the parent has or is taking voluntary steps will not prevent the making of an order, though the English guidance notes that if parents are ready to engage fully with voluntary support an order would not usually be desirable (Home Office/Youth Justice Board/Department for Constitutional Affairs, *Parenting Contracts and Orders Guidance*, February 2004, para.5.10). One example where a parenting order might be made regardless of an indication of voluntary engagement would be in a case where previous voluntary arrangements had not been kept to by the parent.

The Scottish guidance is in slightly different terms, providing that: "Ministers are clear that parenting orders should only be imposed where a parent has been offered support on a voluntary basis and has refused to engage with that support and where their behaviour is having a negative impact on their child." (*Guidance on Parenting Orders*, para.10) Despite this, there would still seem to be no reason why an order should not be made when there was reason to doubt the commitment of the parents to these voluntary measures.

Account to be taken of religion, work and education

110.—(1) A court shall ensure that the requirements of a parenting order made by it avoid, so far as practicable—

(a) any conflict with the religious beliefs of the person specified in the order; and

(b) any interference with times at which that person normally works (or carries out voluntary work) or attends an educational establishment.

(2) The supervising officer appointed by a local authority in respect of a parenting order shall ensure that the directions given by the officer avoid, so far as practicable, the matters mentioned in subsection (1)(a) and (b).

DEFINITIONS
"parenting order":   s.103(1)

Miscellaneous

Restriction on reporting proceedings relating to parenting orders

111.—(1) Subject to subsection (2), a person shall be guilty of an offence if the person publishes, anywhere in the world, any matter in respect of relevant proceedings which is intended, or likely to, identify—

(a) the parent concerned in the proceedings (the "person concerned");

(b) any address as being that of the person concerned;

(c) the child concerned in the proceedings;

(d) any other child—

    (i) who is a member of the same household as the person concerned; or

    (ii) of whom the person concerned is a parent; or

(e) any—

    (i) address; or

    (ii) school,

as being that of a child mentioned in paragraph (c) or (d).

(2) In relevant proceedings, the court may, in the interests of justice, order that subsection (1) shall not apply to the proceedings to such extent as the court considers appropriate.

(3) A person guilty of an offence under subsection (1) shall be liable on summary conviction to a fine not exceeding level 4 on the standard scale.

(4) It shall be a defence for a person charged with an offence under subsection (1) to show that the person—

(a) did not know; and

(b) had no reason to suspect,

that the published matter was intended, or was likely, to identify the person concerned, child, address or school (as the case may be).

(5) Section 46 of the Children and Young Persons (Scotland) Act 1937 (c.37) shall apply in relation to relevant proceedings only in respect of a person concerned in the proceedings as a witness.

(6) A child in whose interests a parenting order has been made shall be regarded as a person who falls within subsection (1)(a) of section 47 of the Criminal Procedure (Scotland) Act 1995 (c.46) for the purposes of that section in its application to proceedings in respect of the commission of an offence under section 107(1) in respect of that order.

(7) In this section—

"programme service" has the meaning given by section 201 of the Broadcasting Act 1990 (c.42);

"publishes" includes—

    (a) causing to be published; and

    (b) publishing in a programme service,

and "published" shall be construed accordingly; and

"relevant proceedings" means—

    (a) proceedings before a sheriff for the purpose of consid-
        ering whether to make a parenting order under section
        13(1);

    (b) proceedings before a sheriff on an application for the
        making of a parenting order under section 102(1);

    (c) proceedings before a sheriff on an application for the
        variation, or revocation, of a parenting order under
        section 105(1);

    (d) proceedings before a sheriff for the purpose of consid-
        ering whether to make an order under section 105(5);

    (e) an appeal arising from proceedings such as are men-
        tioned in paragraphs (a) to (d).

DEFINITIONS

"child":	s.117
"parent":	s.117
"parenting order":	s.103(1)
"publishes":	subs.(7)
"relevant proceedings":	subs.(7)

GENERAL NOTE

The wide scope of this section should be noted. It covers publication anywhere in the world. Arguably omitting this provision would have nullified the protection offered by this section as material could be published on the web overseas, but still be accessible in Scotland.

Conduct of proceedings by reporters

112.—(1) The Scottish Ministers may by regulations empower a reporter, whether or not the reporter is an advocate or solicitor, to conduct proceedings—

    (a) before a sheriff—

       (i) on an application by the Principal Reporter for the making of a parenting order;

      (ii) on an application for the variation, or revocation, of a parenting order made on the application of the Principal Reporter, under section 105(1); or

      (iii) for the purpose of considering whether to make an order under section 105(5) in respect of a parenting order made on the application of the Principal Reporter; or

    (b) before a sheriff principal, on any appeal arising from proceedings such as are mentioned in paragraph (a).

(2) Regulations under subsection (1) may prescribe such requirements as the Scottish Ministers think fit as to—

    (a) qualifications;

    (b) training; or

    (c) experience,

necessary for a reporter to be so empowered.

(3) In this section, "reporter" means—

    (a) the Principal Reporter; and

    (b) any officer of the Scottish Children's Reporter Administration to whom there is delegated, under section 131(1) of the Local Government etc. (Scotland) Act 1994 (c.39), any of the functions which the Principal Reporter has under any enactment.

GENERAL NOTE

As with proceedings under the Children (Scotland) Act 1995 the Reporter will be entitled to conduct certain cases whether or not they are legally qualified.

Initial investigations by Principal Reporter

113.—(1) For the purpose of determining whether to make an application for the making of a parenting order under section 102, the Principal Reporter may make such investigations as the Principal Reporter considers appropriate.

(2) On a request made by the Principal Reporter for the purpose mentioned in subsection (1), a local authority shall supply to the Principal Reporter a report on—

(a) the child in relation to whom the Principal Reporter is determining whether to make the application;

(b) the parent in relation to whom the Principal Reporter is determining whether to make the application; and

(c) such circumstances concerning—
   (i) the child; and
   (ii) the parent,
   as appear to the Principal Reporter to be relevant.

DEFINITIONS
"child": s.117
"parent": s.117
"parenting order": s.103(1)

GENERAL NOTE

This section sets out an obligation on the Reporter to carry out an investigation before deciding whether to apply for a parenting order, and, in subs.(2), the obligations of the local authority to provide the Reporter with information to allow that investigation to be carried out. Section 139 on the sharing of information will also be relevant here.

Power of court to direct Principal Reporter to consider application for parenting order

114. Where, in any proceedings (other than proceedings under section 4 or 102), it appears to a court that it might be appropriate for a parenting order to be made in respect of a parent of a child, the court may require the Principal Reporter to consider whether to apply under section 102 for such an order.

DEFINITIONS
"child": s.117
"parent": s.117
"parenting order": s.103(1)

Guidance about parenting orders

115. A person (other than a court) shall, in discharging functions by virtue of section 13 or this Part, have regard to any guidance given by the Scottish Ministers about—

(a) the discharge of those functions; and

(b) matters arising in connection with the discharge of those functions.

GENERAL NOTE

This guidance, *Guidance on Parenting Orders*, is available at: http://www.scotland.gov.uk/Resource/Doc/37432/0011355.pdf

Power of hearing to direct Principal Reporter to consider application for parenting order

116. After section 75 of the Children (Scotland) Act 1995 (c.36) there shall be inserted—

"Parenting orders

Requirement on Principal Reporter to consider application for parenting order

75A.—(1) Subsection (2) below applies where it appears to—

(a) the children's hearing to whom a child's case has been referred under section 65(1) of this Act; or

(b) a children's hearing arranged, under section 73(8) of this Act, to review a supervision requirement in respect of a child,

that it might be appropriate for a parenting order to be made in respect of a parent of the child under section 102 of the Antisocial Behaviour etc. (Scotland) Act 2004 (asp 8) (the "2004 Act").

(2) The hearing may require the Principal Reporter to consider whether to apply, under subsection (3) of that section of the 2004 Act, for such an order.

(3) A requirement under subsection (2) above shall specify—

(a) the parent in respect of whom it might be appropriate for the order to be made; and

(b) by reference to subsections (4) to (6) of that section of the 2004 Act, the condition in respect of which the application might be made.

(4) In subsection (1) above, "parent" and "child" have the same meanings as in section 117 of the 2004 Act.".

DEFINITIONS
"child":   s.117
"parent":   s.117
"parenting order":   s.103(1)

GENERAL NOTE
A children's hearing, whether considering a referral for the first time or conducting a review of an existing supervision requirement, can require the Reporter to consider whether to apply for a parenting order. Before doing this the hearing must consider that such an order might be appropriate. The requirement must set out the parent in respect of whom the application is to be made and the ground on which the application might be made, *i.e.* is the hearing of the opinion that the behaviour condition, the conduct condition or the welfare condition set out in s.102 is satisfied in relation to the child. Where such a requirement is made the Reporter will have discretion to decide whether or not to actually make the application.

Interpretation

Interpretation of Part 9

117. In this Part—

"child" means a person who is under the age of 16 years;

"parent", means any individual who is a relevant person as defined in section 93(2)(b) of the Children (Scotland) Act 1995 (c.36) (the references to a "person" in that section being read as references to an individual);

"parenting order" has the meaning given by section 103(1).

GENERAL NOTE
The definition of parent is a broad one and covers not only individuals with parental responsibilities and rights in relation to a child, but also those without such responsibilities and rights who have actual charge or control of the child. It will therefore include, for example, unmarried fathers who do not automatically have parental responsibilities and rights provided that they have some responsibility for the care of the child.

PART 10

FURTHER CRIMINAL MEASURES

Antisocial behaviour orders

Antisocial behaviour orders
118. After section 234A of the Criminal Procedure (Scotland) Act 1995 (c.46) there shall be inserted—

"Antisocial behaviour orders

Antisocial behaviour orders
234AA.—(1) Where subsection (2) below applies, the court may, instead of or in addition to imposing any sentence which it could impose, make an antisocial behaviour order in respect of a person (the "offender").
(2) This subsection applies where—
(a) the offender is convicted of an offence;
(b) at the time when he committed the offence, the offender was at least 12 years of age;
(c) in committing the offence, he engaged in antisocial behaviour; and
(d) the court is satisfied, on a balance of probabilities, that the making of an antisocial behaviour order is necessary for the purpose of protecting other persons from further antisocial behaviour by the offender.
(3) For the purposes of subsection (2)(c) above, a person engages in antisocial behaviour if he—
(a) acts in a manner that causes or is likely to cause alarm or distress; or
(b) pursues a course of conduct that causes or is likely to cause alarm or distress,
to at least one person who is not of the same household as him.
(4) Subject to subsection (5) below, an antisocial behaviour order is an order which prohibits, indefinitely or for such period as may be specified in the order, the offender from doing anything described in the order.
(5) The prohibitions that may be imposed by an antisocial behaviour order are those necessary for the purpose of protecting other persons from further antisocial behaviour by the offender.
(6) Before making an antisocial behaviour order, the court shall explain to the offender in ordinary language—
(a) the effect of the order and the prohibitions proposed to be included in it;
(b) the consequences of failing to comply with the order;
(c) the powers the court has under subsection (8) below; and
(d) the entitlement of the offender to appeal against the making of the order.
(7) Failure to comply with subsection (6) shall not affect the validity of the order.
(8) On the application of the offender in respect of whom an antisocial behaviour order is made under this section, the court which made the order may, if satisfied on a balance of probabilities that it is appropriate to do so—

(a) revoke the order; or

(b) subject to subsection (9) below, vary it in such manner as it thinks fit.

(9) Where an antisocial behaviour order specifies a period, the court may not, under subsection (8)(b) above, vary the order by extending the period.

(10) An antisocial behaviour order made under this section, and any revocation or variation of such an order under subsection (8) above, shall be taken to be a sentence for the purposes of an appeal.

(11) Sections 9 and 11 of the Antisocial Behaviour etc. (Scotland) Act 2004 (asp 8) (which provide that breach of an antisocial behaviour order made under that Act is an offence for which a person is liable to be arrested without warrant) shall apply in relation to antisocial behaviour orders made under this section as those sections apply in relation to antisocial behaviour orders made under section 4 of that Act.

(12) In this section, "conduct" includes speech; and a course of conduct must involve conduct on at least two occasions.

Antisocial behaviour orders: notification

234AB.—(1) Upon making an antisocial behaviour order under section 234AA of this Act, the court shall—

(a) serve a copy of the order on the offender; and

(b) give a copy of the order to the local authority it considers most appropriate.

(2) Upon revoking an antisocial behaviour order under subsection (8)(a) of that section, the court shall notify the local authority to whom a copy of the order was given under subsection (1)(b) above.

(3) Upon varying an antisocial behaviour order under subsection (8)(b) of that section, the court shall—

(a) serve a copy of the order as varied on the offender; and

(b) give a copy of the order as varied to the local authority to whom a copy of the order was given under subsection (1)(b) above.

(4) For the purposes of this section, a copy is served on an offender if—

(a) given to him; or

(b) sent to him by registered post or the recorded delivery service.

(5) A certificate of posting of a letter sent under subsection (4)(b) issued by the postal operator shall be sufficient evidence of the sending of the letter on the day specified in such certificate.

(6) In this section, "offender" means the person in respect of whom the antisocial behaviour order was made.".

GENERAL NOTE

These provisions confer on criminal courts the power to make an antisocial behaviour order either instead of or in addition to any other sentence imposed on conviction. Before the power can be exercised the offence must have involved the offender engaging in antisocial behaviour and the order must be necessary to protect others from antisocial behaviour. The standard of proof to be satisfied in establishing the necessity for the order is the balance of probabilities. This seems slightly at odds with the views expressed by the courts in relation to an application for an ASBO under s.4 that whether an order is necessary involves an exercise of judgement and not a standard of proof, see General Note to s.4.

Once an order has been made it can be varied or discharged on the application of the offender made to the court which made the order. The only restriction on the powers of variation is that the order cannot be extended, though in the case of indefinite orders this will not be an issue. The case for variation or discharge has to be established on the balance of probabilities. Notification of the order has to be made not only to the offender, but also to the authority which the court considers most relevant. This need not be the authority of the offender's residence, but may be the authority for the area where it is likely that future antisocial behaviour will take place.

Records of antisocial behaviour orders made in criminal courts

119.—(1) A local authority shall keep records of each antisocial behaviour order of which the authority has been given a copy by virtue of subsection (1)(b) of section 234AB of the Criminal Procedure (Scotland) Act 1995 (c.46) (the "1995 Act").

(2) A record kept under subsection (1) shall specify—
(a) the person in respect of whom the order was made;
(b) the prohibitions imposed by the order;
(c) whether a prohibition is indefinite or for a definite period and where it is for a period, that period;
(d) where the authority is, by virtue of subsection (2) of that section of the 1995 Act, notified of the revocation of the order, the date on which it was revoked;
(e) where the authority is, by virtue of subsection (3)(b) of that section of the 1995 Act, given a copy of the order as varied, the variation and its date; and
(f) such other matters relating to the order as the Scottish Ministers may prescribe in regulations.

(3) A local authority shall, on a request to do so being made to it by a person mentioned in subsection (4), disclose to that person information contained in a record kept under subsection (1).

(4) Those persons are—
(a) the Scottish Ministers;
(b) the Principal Reporter;
(c) any other local authority;
(d) a chief constable; and
(e) a registered social landlord.

(5) A local authority shall, in discharging functions by virtue of this section, have regard to such guidance issued by the Scottish Ministers as to—
(a) the discharge of those functions; and
(b) such matters arising in connection with the discharge of those functions,
as the Scottish Ministers think fit.

GENERAL NOTE
As is the case with antisocial behaviour orders made under s.4 (see s.15) the local authority must maintain a register of orders notified to them. Although subss (3)—(4) suggest that information from the register should be disclosed on the request of one of those listed in subs.(4), the guidance issued by the Scottish Executive suggests that in some cases this information should be passed on without a request. In particular it suggests that where an authority is aware that an individual plans to or has moved to a different authority area it should pass on any information about any antisocial behaviour order granted against the individual to the local authority for that area (*Guidance on Antisocial Behaviour Orders*, para.147). It is also suggested that registered social landlords are kept informed of any orders made by a criminal court which might be relevant to them.

Community reparation orders

Community reparation orders

120. After section 245J of the Criminal Procedure (Scotland) Act 1995 (c.46) there shall be inserted—

"Community reparation orders

Community reparation orders

245K.—(1) Where subsection (2) below applies, the court may, instead of imposing any sentence which, but for this subsection, it could impose, make a community reparation order in respect of a person ("the offender").

(2) This subsection applies where—

(a) the offender is convicted in summary proceedings of an offence;

(b) at the time when he committed the offence, he was at least 12 years old;

(c) he committed the offence by engaging to any extent in antisocial behaviour; and

(d) in relation to the local authority that would be specified in the order, the Scottish Ministers have notified the court that the authority has made arrangements that would enable an order to be complied with.

(3) For the purposes of subsection (2)(c) above, a person engages in antisocial behaviour if he—

(a) acts in a manner that causes or is likely to cause alarm or distress; or

(b) pursues a course of conduct that causes or is likely to cause alarm or distress,

to at least one person who is not of the same household as him.

(4) A community reparation order is an order—

(a) requiring the specified local authority to appoint a supervising officer for the purposes of—

(i) determining which prescribed activities the offender should undertake for the specified number of hours (being at least 10 and not exceeding 100) during the period of 12 months beginning with the day on which the order is made;

(ii) determining at what times and in which localities he should undertake those activities; and

(iii) giving the offender directions during that period to undertake activities in accordance with determinations under sub-paragraphs (i) and (ii) above; and

(b) requiring the offender, during that period, to comply with those directions.

(5) In subsection (4) above—

"prescribed activities" means activities designed—

(a) to enable reparation to be made (whether to a particular person or to a group of persons and whether such a person, or any person in the group, has been affected by the antisocial behaviour or otherwise) by persons who have engaged in antisocial behaviour; or

(b) to reduce the likelihood of persons engaging in such behaviour, which are of such description as the Scottish Ministers may by regulations prescribe; and

"specified" means specified in the order.

(6) The Scottish Ministers may by regulations make provision about determinations made, and directions given, by virtue of paragraph (a) of subsection (4) above.

(7) In giving directions by virtue of subsection (4)(a)(iii) above, a supervising officer shall, as far as practicable, avoid—

(a) any conflict with the offender's religious beliefs;
(b) any interference with the times at which the offender normally works (or carries out voluntary work) or attends an educational establishment.

(8) Before making a community reparation order in respect of an offender, the court shall explain to him in ordinary language—
(a) the purpose and effect of the order;
(b) the consequences of failure to comply with the order; and
(c) the powers the court has under section 245P of this Act.

(9) For the purposes of any appeal or review, a community reparation order is a sentence.

(10) Regulations under subsections (5) and (6) above shall be made by statutory instrument; and any such instrument shall be subject to annulment in pursuance of a resolution of the Scottish Parliament.

Community reparation order: notification
245L. Where the court makes a community reparation order it shall intimate the making of the order to—
(a) the offender;
(b) the chief social work officer of the local authority specified in the order; and
(c) where it is not the appropriate court, the clerk of the appropriate court.

Failure to comply with community reparation order: extension of 12 month period
245M. Subject to sections 245N(4) and 245P(2)(c) and (d) of this Act, if—
(a) a community reparation order is made in respect of an offender; and
(b) the offender fails to comply with a direction given by the supervising officer appointed by virtue of the order,
then the order shall, notwithstanding section 245K(4)(a)(i), remain in force until the offender has complied with the direction.

Failure to comply with community reparation order: powers of court
245N.—(1) Subsection (2) below applies where—
(a) a community reparation order is made in respect of an offender; and
(b) on information from the offender's supervising officer, it appears to the appropriate court that the offender has failed to comply with the order or any direction given under it.

(2) The court may issue—
(a) a warrant for the arrest of the offender; or
(b) a citation requiring the offender to appear before the court at such time as may be specified in the citation.

(3) The unified citation provisions shall apply in relation to a citation under this section as they apply in relation to a citation under section 216(3)(a) of this Act.

(4) If it is proved to the satisfaction of the court before which the offender is brought or appears in pursuance of subsection (2) above that the offender has failed without reasonable excuse to comply with the order or any direction given under it, the court may revoke the order and deal with the offender in any manner in which he could

have been dealt with for the original offence if the order had not been made.

(5) The evidence of one witness shall, for the purposes of subsection (4) above, be sufficient evidence.

Extension, variation and revocation of order

245P.—(1) Subsection (2) below applies where a community reparation order is made in respect of an offender.

(2) On the application of the offender or the offender's supervising officer, the appropriate court may, if it appears to it that it would be in the interests of justice to do so having regard to circumstances which have arisen since the order was made—

(a) extend, in relation to the order, the period of 12 months specified in section 245K(4)(a)(i) of this Act;

(b) vary the numbers of hours specified in the order;

(c) revoke the order; or

(d) revoke the order and deal with the offender in any manner in which he could have been dealt with for the original offence if the order had not been made.

(3) If the court proposes to exercise its powers under subsection (2)(a), (b) or (d) above otherwise than on the application of the offender, it shall issue a citation requiring the offender to appear before the court at such time as may be specified in the citation and, if he fails to appear, may issue a warrant for his arrest.

(4) The unified citation provisions shall apply in relation to a citation under this section as they apply in relation to a citation under section 216(3)(a) of this Act.

Sections 245L, 245N and 245P: meaning of "appropriate court"

245Q. In sections 245L, 245N and 245P of this Act, "appropriate court", in relation to a community reparation order, means the court having jurisdiction in the area of the local authority specified in the order, being a sheriff or district court according to whether the order is made by a sheriff or district court (except that, in the case where an order is made by a district court and there is no district court in that area, it means the sheriff).".

GENERAL NOTE

The section introduces a new community penalty available only to summary courts. It will be available for anyone aged 12 or over whose offence has involved engaging in antisocial behaviour 'to any extent'. Subject to meeting the threshold implied in the definition of antisocial behaviour in subs.(3) it appears that the antisocial behaviour element in the offence could be minimal.

The order requites the offender to be under the supervision of a local authority officer for between 10 and 100 hours with a view to undertaking activities ('prescribed activities') designed either to make reparation to the community or to reduce the likelihood of the offender behaving in an antisocial manner. Reparation need not be directly related to the offender's antisocial behaviour, nor need it be directed to benefit victims of antisocial behaviour in general. The activities will normally be completed within 12 months, but the order will automatically be extended until the requirements of the supervising officer have been complied with.

The Community Reparation Orders (Requirements for Consultation and Prescribed Activities) (Scotland) Regulations 2005 (SSI 2005/18) sets out four types of activities which can be prescribed as part of a community reparation order. Aside from work providing reparation for the community affected, these are programmes (a) to raise awareness about the offender's offending behaviour, (b) to reduce future offending and antisocial behaviour, and (c) to encourage personal and social responsibility (reg.3).

During the passage of the Act the point was made that the objective of community reparation could already be achieved in respect of children between 12 and 15 because of the wide powers of children's hearings to attach conditions to a supervision requirement.

Restriction of liberty orders

Restriction of liberty orders

121.—(1) Section 245A of the Criminal Procedure (Scotland) Act 1995 (c.46) (restriction of liberty orders) shall be amended in accordance with subsections (2) and (3).

(2) In subsection (1), the words "of 16 years of age or more" are repealed.

(3) After subsection (11), there shall be inserted—

"(11A) A court shall not make a restriction of liberty order in respect of an offender who is under 16 years of age unless, having obtained a report on the offender from the local authority in whose area he resides, it is satisfied as to the services which the authority will provide for his support and rehabilitation during the period when he is subject to the order.".

GENERAL NOTE

The effect of his section is to remove the lower age limit for the imposition by a criminal court of a restriction of liberty order. Orders imposed on anyone under the age of 16 will, however, have two significant differences from the normal restriction of liberty order. In the first place it will be necessary for the court to obtain a report from the local authority on the offender before making this order. Secondly, the local authority will normally be expected to offer services to provide support and rehabilitation during the period of the order. This contrasts with orders made on those aged 16 or over which contain no such input.

Sale of spray paint to children

Offence of selling spray paint to child

122.—(1) A person who sells to a person under the age of 16 a spray paint device shall be guilty of an offence.

(2) In subsection (1), "spray paint device" means a device which—

(a) contains paint stored under pressure; and

(b) is designed to permit the release of the paint as a spray.

(3) A person guilty of an offence under subsection (1) shall be liable on summary conviction to a fine not exceeding level 3 on the standard scale.

(4) It shall be a defence for a person charged with an offence under subsection (1) to show that the person took all reasonable precautions and exercised all due diligence to avoid the commission of the offence.

DEFINITIONS

"spray paint device":　　　　　　　subs.(2)

GENERAL NOTE

This section is designed to tackle graffiti problems by restricting the sale of spray paints to those under 16. How effective it is in achieving this goal remains to be seen given the wide variety of other types of marker used to graffiti surfaces. It is a defence that all reasonable precautions were taken and that all due diligence was exercised to avoid selling to someone under 16.

Requirement to display warning statement

123.—(1) A notice displaying the statement—

"It is illegal to sell a spray paint device to anyone under the age of 16" shall be exhibited at an appropriate place at every premises at which spray paint devices are sold by retail.

(2) In subsection (1), "appropriate place" means a prominent position where the statement is readily visible to persons at the point of sale of spray paint devices.

(3) The dimensions of the notice to be exhibited in accordance with subsection (1), and the size of the statement to be displayed on it, shall be such as may be prescribed by regulations made by the Scottish Ministers.

(4) Where—

(a) a person carries on a business involving the retail of spray paint devices at any premises; and

(b) no notice is exhibited in accordance with subsection (1) at those premises,

that person shall be guilty of an offence.

(5) A person guilty of an offence under subsection (4) shall be liable on summary conviction to a fine not exceeding level 2 on the standard scale.

(6) It shall be a defence for a person charged with an offence under subsection (4) to show that the person took all reasonable precautions and exercised all due diligence to avoid the commission of the offence.

(7) Where an offence under subsection (4) is committed by a body corporate and is proved to have been committed with the consent or connivance of, or to be attributable to, any neglect on the part of, any director, manager, secretary or other similar officer of the body corporate or any person who was purporting to act in any such capacity, that person as well as the body corporate shall be guilty of that offence.

(8) In subsection (7), "director", in relation to a body corporate whose affairs are managed by its members, means a member of the body corporate.

(9) Where an offence under subsection (4) is committed by a Scottish partnership and is proved to have been committed with the consent or connivance of, or to be attributable to any neglect on the part of, a partner, that partner as well as the partnership shall be guilty of that offence.

(10) In this section—

"premises" includes—

(a) any place; and

(b) any vehicle, vessel, aircraft, hovercraft, stall or moveable structure; and

"spray paint device" has (except where it appears in the statement set out in subsection (1)) the same meaning as in section 122(1).

DEFINITIONS
"premises":   subs.(10)
"spray paint device":   s.122(2)

GENERAL NOTE
The dimensions of the required notice and the size of the lettering required are set out in the Sale of Spray Paint (Display of Warning Statement) (Scotland) Regulations 2004 (SSI 2004/419).

Offences under sections 122 and 123: enforcement

124.—(1) A local authority shall, within its area, enforce sections 122 and 123.

(2) Subsection (1) does not authorise a local authority to institute proceedings for an offence under section 122(1) or 123(4).

GENERAL NOTE
The main responsibility for enforcing the ban on sales of spray paint and the requirement to display a warning notice lies with the local authority, though any decision to prosecute and

consequential prosecution will be a matter for the procurator fiscal. Police officers will also be able to enforce these provisions.

Offences under sections 122 and 123: powers of entry, inspection and seizure

125.—(1) Subject to subsection (3), an authorised officer of a local authority may at any reasonable hour exercise any of the powers conferred by subsections (4) to (7).

(2) In subsection (1), "authorised officer", in relation to a local authority, means an officer of the authority authorised in writing by it for the purposes of this section.

(3) An officer seeking to exercise a power mentioned in subsection (1) shall, if requested, produce evidence of identity and authorisation.

(4) The officer may, for the purpose of ascertaining whether a relevant offence has been committed—

(a) inspect any goods; and

(b) enter any premises (other than premises used only as a dwelling).

(5) If the officer has reasonable cause to suspect that a relevant offence has been committed, the officer may, for the purpose of ascertaining whether it has been committed—

(a) require any person carrying on, or employed in connection with, a business, to produce any records relating to the business; and

(b) take copies of, or of any entry in, any records produced by virtue of paragraph (a).

(6) If the officer has reasonable cause to believe that a relevant offence has been committed, the officer may, for the purpose of ascertaining, by testing or otherwise, whether it has been committed, seize and detain any goods.

(7) The officer may seize and detain any goods or records which the officer has reason to believe may be required as evidence in proceedings for a relevant offence.

(8) In this section, "relevant offence" means an offence under section 122(1) or 123(4).

DEFINITIONS
"authorised officer":   subs.(2)
"relevant offence":   subs.(8)

GENERAL NOTE

Although this section gives powers of entry, inspection and seizure, it does not specifically provide for the use of test purchases by children under 16 as a means of enforcement. These will, instead, be governed by guidance issued by the Lord Advocate (Scottish Executive, *Guidance on Ban on Sale of Spray Paint to Under 16s*, para.18, available at: http://www.scotland.gov.uk/library5/social/asbp.pdf)

Seizure of vehicles

Vehicles used in manner causing alarm, distress or annoyance

126.—(1) Where—

(a) regulations under section 127 are in force; and

(b) subsection (2) applies,

a constable in uniform may exercise the powers mentioned in subsection (3).

(2) This subsection applies where the constable has reasonable grounds for believing that a motor vehicle—

    (a) is being used on any occasion in a manner which—
        (i) contravenes section 3 or 34 of the Road Traffic Act 1988 (c.52) (careless and inconsiderate driving and prohibition of off-road driving); and
        (ii) is causing, or is likely to cause, alarm, distress or annoyance to members of the public; or
    (b) has been used on any occasion in a manner which—
        (i) contravened either of those sections of that Act; and
        (ii) caused, or was likely to cause, such alarm, distress or annoyance.

(3) The powers are—

    (a) if the motor vehicle is moving, power to order the person driving it to stop the vehicle;

    (b) subject to subsection (4), power to seize and remove the motor vehicle;

    (c) for the purposes of exercising a power falling within paragraph (a) or (b), power to enter any premises (other than a private dwelling house) on which the constable has reasonable grounds for believing the motor vehicle to be;

    (d) power to use reasonable force, if necessary, in the exercise of a power conferred by any of paragraphs (a) to (c).

(4) Subject to subsection (5), the constable shall not seize the motor vehicle unless—

    (a) where the case falls within subsection (2)(a)—
        (i) the constable has warned the person who is using the motor vehicle in the manner mentioned in that subsection that if the use continues the constable will seize the vehicle; and
        (ii) it appears to the constable that, after the warning, the use has continued; or

    (b) where the case falls within subsection (2)(b)—
        (i) the constable has warned the person who used the motor vehicle in the manner mentioned in that subsection that if the use is repeated, the constable will seize the vehicle; and
        (ii) it appears to the constable that, after the warning, the use has been repeated.

(5) Subsection (4) does not require a warning to be given by a constable on any occasion on which the constable would otherwise have the power to seize a motor vehicle under this section if—

    (a) the circumstances make it impracticable for the constable to give the warning;

    (b) the constable has already on that occasion given a warning under that subsection in respect of any use of that motor vehicle or of another motor vehicle by that person or any other person; or

    (c) the constable has reasonable grounds for believing—
        (i) that such a warning has been given on that occasion otherwise than by that constable; or
        (ii) that the person whose use of that motor vehicle on that occasion would justify the seizure is a person to whom a warning under that subsection has been given (whether or not by that constable or in respect of the same vehicle or the same or a similar use) on a previous occasion in the previous 12 months.

(6) A person who fails to comply with an order under subsection (3)(a) shall be guilty of an offence.

(7) A person guilty of an offence under subsection (6) shall be liable on summary conviction to a fine not exceeding level 3 on the standard scale.

(8) In this section—

"driving" has the same meaning as in the Road Traffic Act 1988 (c.52);

"motor vehicle" means any mechanically propelled vehicle, whether or not it is intended or adapted for use on roads; and

"private dwelling house" does not include—

(a) any garage or other structure occupied with the dwelling house; or

(b) any land appurtenant to the dwelling house.

DEFINITIONS

"driving":	subs.(8)
"motor vehicle":	subs.(8)
"private dwelling house":	subs.(8)

GENERAL NOTE

This section and the following section together provide a scheme to tackle those who make antisocial use of their vehicles. The specific problem giving rise to these provisions (introduced at stage 3 by the MSP for Springburn, Paul Martin) was the use of quad bikes and trail bikes on open ground and public parks in a way which both caused annoyance and was also potentially dangerous to other users of the land.

The provisions of this section will only apply where regulations have been made under s.127 providing for the removal, retention, release and disposal of vehicles seized under the powers conferred here. These regulations, The Police (Retention and Disposal of Motor Vehicles) (Scotland) Regulations 2005 (SSI 2005/80), came into force on March 17, 2005.

A two stage process is set out. The first stage is a warning given to someone who is using or has used their vehicle in a way which contravenes either s.3 or s.34 of the Road Traffic Act 1988 (c.52) and causes or is likely to cause alarm, distress or annoyance. The sections of the Road Traffic Act 1988 referred to make it an offence to drive without due care and attention or without reasonable consideration for others (s.3) and to drive otherwise than on a road (s.4). Police officers will therefore be enabled to issue a warning if a vehicle is used in this way either on the road or on open ground. The warning will need to specifically refer to the possibility of seizure of the vehicle if the person continues driving in the same manner.

If, despite the warning, the antisocial use of the vehicle is repeated the vehicle can then be seized. This seizure need not be immediate. In certain circumstances seizure can take place without a prior warning (subs.(5)), these include circumstances where it would be impracticable to give a warning or where a warning has already been given in respect of another vehicle.

Retention etc. of vehicles seized under section 126

127.—(1) The Scottish Ministers may by regulations make provision as to—

(a) the removal and retention of motor vehicles seized under section 126; and

(b) the release or disposal of such vehicles.

(2) Regulations under subsection (1) may in particular make provision for or in connection with—

(a) the giving of notice of the seizure of a motor vehicle under section 126 to a person who—

(i) is the owner of that vehicle; or

(ii) in accordance with the regulations, appears to be its owner;

(b) the procedure by which a person who claims to be the owner of a motor vehicle seized under section 126 may seek to have it released;

(c) requiring the payment of fees, charges or other costs in relation to—

(i) the removal and retention of such a motor vehicle; and

(ii) any application for its release;

(d) the circumstances in which a motor vehicle seized under section 126 may be disposed of;

(e) the delivery to a local authority, in circumstances prescribed by or determined in accordance with the regulations, of any motor vehicle seized under section 126.

(3) Regulations under subsection (1) shall provide that a person who would otherwise be liable to pay any fee or charge under the regulations shall not be liable to pay it if—

(a) the use by reference to which the motor vehicle concerned was seized was not a use by that person; and

(b) the person—
   (i) did not know of the use of the vehicle in the manner that led to its seizure;
   (ii) had not consented to its use in that manner; and
   (iii) could not, by the taking of reasonable steps, have prevented its use in that manner.

(4) In this section, "motor vehicle" has the same meaning as in section 126.

DEFINITIONS
"motor vehicle":   s.126(8)

GENERAL NOTE
This section provides for the making of regulations regarding the retention, release and disposal of vehicles seized in exercise of the powers conferred by s.126. These regulations, The Police (Retention and Disposal of Motor Vehicles) (Scotland) Regulations 2005 (SSI 2005/80), came into force on March 17, 2005.

PART 11

FIXED PENALTIES

GENERAL NOTE
This part of the Act confers extensive powers on police officers to serve fixed penalty notices on a wide range of offences which might fall into the antisocial category. The stated objective of this is to free up police time and reduce the burden on courts (in terms of s.131 the case will only get to court if the person served with the notice requests a trial). The scheme is being piloted in the Tayside combined police area (The Antisocial Behaviour (Fixed Penalty Offence) (Prescribed Area) (Scotland) Regulations 2005 (SSI 2005/106)).
In addition, further guidance on the use of notices will be issued by the Lord Advocate to clarify those offences in respect of which use of a fixed penalty would be appropriate. For example, the common law offence of Breach of the Peace covers a very wide variety of behaviour from the trivial to the potentially very serious and guidance will be required on which cases are appropriate for the use of a fixed penalty.

Offences to which this Part applies

Fixed penalty offences
128.—(1) For the purposes of this Part "fixed penalty offence" means—

(a) an offence under an enactment mentioned in the first column in Part 1 of the following table and described, in general terms, in the second column in that Part;

(b) an offence created in subordinate legislation made under an enactment mentioned in the first column in Part 2 of the table which is of the general description mentioned in the second column in that Part; and

(c) a common law offence mentioned in Part 3 of the table.

TABLE

PART 1	
Enactment	*Description of offence*
Section 78 of the Licensing (Scotland) Act 1976 (c.66)	Riotous behaviour while drunk in licensed premises
Section 79 of the Licensing (Scotland) Act 1976 (c.66)	Refusing to leave licensed premises on being requested to do so
Section 47 of the Civic Government (Scotland) Act 1982 (c.45)	Urinating or defecating in circumstances causing annoyance to others
Section 50(1) of the Civic Government (Scotland) Act 1982 (c.45)	Being drunk and incapable in a public place
Section 50(2) of the Civic Government (Scotland) Act 1982 (c.45)	Being drunk in a public place in charge of a child
Section 54(1) of the Civic Government (Scotland) Act 1982 (c.45)	Persisting, to annoyance of others, in playing musical instruments, singing, playing radios etc. on being required to stop
Section 52(1) of the Criminal Law (Consolidation) (Scotland) Act 1995 (c.39)	Vandalism

PART 2	
Enactment	*Description of offence*
Sections 201 and 203 of the Local Government (Scotland) Act 1973 (c.65)	Consuming alcoholic liquor in a public Place

PART 3
Common law offence
Breach of the peace
Malicious mischief

(2) The Scottish Ministers may by order—
(a) amend an entry in the table;
(b) add an entry to the table;
(c) remove an entry from the table.
(3) An order under subsection (2) may make such amendment of any provision of this Part as the Scottish Ministers consider appropriate in consequence of any amendment of, or addition to or removal from, the table made by the order.

DEFINITIONS
"fixed penalty offence":   subs.(1)

GENERAL NOTE
This section sets out a list of offences in respect of which a police officer can issue a fixed penalty notice under s.129. As noted in the General Note to this Part, further guidance will be given to the police as to the offences where use of a fixed penalty notice is appropriate.

Fixed penalty notices and penalties

Fixed penalty notices
   129.—(1) A constable who has reason to believe that a person aged 16 or over has committed a fixed penalty offence in a prescribed area may give the person a fixed penalty notice in respect of the offence.
   (2) In subsection (1)—
"fixed penalty notice" means a notice offering the opportunity, by paying a fixed penalty in accordance with this Part, to discharge any liability to be convicted of the offence to which the notice relates; and
"prescribed area" means an area prescribed by the Scottish Ministers by regulations.

DEFINITIONS
"fixed penalty notice":   subs.(2)
"fixed penalty offence":   s.128(1)
"prescribed area":   subs.(2)

GENERAL NOTE
   The power to serve a fixed penalty notice can only be exercised where the area has been prescribed as an area in which the power can be exercised. Currently (June 2005) the only area where the power can be exercised is the Tayside combined police area (The Antisocial Behaviour (Fixed Penalty Offence) (Prescribed Area) (Scotland) Regulations 2005 (SSI 2005/106)).

Amount of fixed penalty and form of fixed penalty notice
   130.—(1) Subject to subsection (2), the penalty payable in respect of a fixed penalty offence is such amount as the Scottish Ministers may specify by order.
   (2) The Scottish Ministers may not specify an amount exceeding level 2 on the standard scale.
   (3) A fixed penalty notice shall—
   (a) state the alleged offence;
   (b) give such particulars of the circumstances alleged to constitute the offence as are necessary to provide reasonable information about it;
   (c) state the amount of the fixed penalty;
   (d) state the clerk of the district court to whom, and the address at which, the fixed penalty may be paid;
   (e) inform the person to whom it is given of the right to ask to be tried for the alleged offence and explain how that right may be exercised; and
   (f) include such other information as the Scottish Ministers may by order prescribe.

DEFINITIONS
"fixed penalty notice":   s.129(2)
"fixed penalty offence":   s.128(1)

GENERAL NOTE
   The amount of the fixed penalty is £40 (The Antisocial Behaviour (Amount of Fixed Penalty) (Scotland) Order 2005 (SSI 2005/110)). On the form of the notice see the Antisocial Behaviour (Fixed Penalty Notice) (Additional Information) (Scotland) Order 2005 (SSI 2005/130).

Effect of fixed penalty notice
   131.—(1) This section applies if a fixed penalty notice is given to a person ("A") under section 129.

(2) Subject to subsection (3), proceedings may not be brought against A.

(3) If A asks to be tried for the alleged offence, proceedings may be brought against A.

(4) Such a request shall be made by a notice given by A—

(a) in the manner specified in the fixed penalty notice; and

(b) before the end of the period of 28 days beginning with the day on which the notice is given.

(5) If, by the end of the period mentioned in paragraph (b) of subsection (4)—

(a) the fixed penalty has not been paid in accordance with this Part; and

(b) A has not made a request in accordance with that subsection,

then A is liable to pay to the clerk of the district court specified in the fixed penalty notice a sum equal to one and a half times the amount of the fixed penalty.

(6) A sum for which A is liable by virtue of subsection (5) shall be treated as if it were a fine imposed by the district court specified in the fixed penalty notice.

DEFINITIONS

"fixed penalty notice": s.129(2)

GENERAL NOTE

A person served with a fixed penalty notice has 28 days either to pay the penalty or to request a trial. If he/she does neither of these within the 28 day period the penalty is automatically increased by one half (subs.(5)) and can then be recovered in the same way as a district court fine (subs.(6)).

Payment of fixed penalty

132.—(1) The fixed penalty stated in a fixed penalty notice is payable to the clerk of the district court specified in the notice.

(2) Payment of the penalty may be made by properly addressing, pre-paying and posting a letter containing the amount of the penalty (in cash or otherwise).

(3) Subsection (4) applies if a person—

(a) claims to have made payment in accordance with subsection (2); and

(b) shows that a letter was posted.

(4) Unless the contrary is proved, payment is to be regarded as being made at the time at which the letter would be delivered in the ordinary course of post.

(5) Subsection (2) is not to be read as preventing the payment of a penalty by other means.

(6) Any sum received by the clerk of a district court by virtue of subsection (1) or section 131(5) shall be treated as if it were a fine imposed by that court.

(7) A letter is properly addressed for the purposes of subsection (2) if it is addressed in accordance with the requirements specified in the fixed penalty notice.

DEFINITIONS

"fixed penalty notice": s.129(2)

Revocation of fixed penalty notices

Revocation of fixed penalty notices

133.—(1) If—

(a) a fixed penalty notice is given to a person under section 129; and
(b) a constable determines that either of the conditions mentioned in subsection (2) is satisfied,
the constable may revoke the notice.
(2) Those conditions are—
(a) that the offence to which the fixed penalty notice relates was not committed; and
(b) that the notice ought not to have been issued to the person named as the person to whom it was issued.
(3) Where a fixed penalty notice is revoked—
(a) no amount shall be payable by way of fixed penalty in pursuance of that notice; and
(b) any amount paid by way of fixed penalty in pursuance of that notice shall be repaid to the person who paid it.

DEFINITIONS
"fixed penalty notice":   s.129(2)

GENERAL NOTE
A fixed penalty notice can be revoked if a constable decides both that the offence was not committed and the notice ought not to have been issued to the person named in it.

Interpretation

Interpretation of Part 11
134. In this Part—
"fixed penalty notice" has the meaning given by section 129(2); and
"fixed penalty offence" has the meaning given in section 128(1).

PART 12

CHILDREN'S HEARINGS

Supervision requirements

Supervision requirements: conditions restricting movement
135.—(1) Section 70 of the Children (Scotland) Act 1995 (c.36) (supervision requirements) shall be amended in accordance with subsections (2) to (4).
(2) For subsection (9) there shall be substituted—
"(9) A children's hearing may exercise a power mentioned in subsection (9A) below in relation to a child if they are satisfied—
(a) that one of the conditions mentioned in subsection (10) below is met; and
(b) that it is necessary to exercise the power concerned.
(9A) The powers are—
(a) that the children's hearing may specify in the supervision requirement that the child shall be liable to be placed and kept in secure accommodation in a residential establishment specified, under subsection (3)(a) above, in the requirement, during such period as the person in charge of that establishment, with the agreement of the chief social work officer of the relevant local authority, considers necessary; and
(b) that the children's hearing may impose, under subsection (3)(b) above, a movement restriction condition.".

(3) For subsection (10) there shall be substituted—
  "(10) The conditions are—
    (a) that the child, having previously absconded, is likely to abscond and, if he absconds, it is likely that his physical, mental or moral welfare will be at risk; and
    (b) that the child is likely to injure himself or some other person.".
(4) After subsection (10) there shall be added—
  "(11) In this section, "movement restriction condition" means a condition—
    (a) restricting the child's movements in such way as may be specified in the supervision requirement; and
    (b) requiring the child to comply with such arrangements for monitoring compliance with the restriction mentioned in paragraph (a) above as may be so specified.
  (12) Where a children's hearing impose a condition such as is mentioned in subsection (9A)(b) above, they shall also impose under subsection (3)(b) above such of the conditions prescribed by the Scottish Ministers for the purposes of this section as they consider necessary in the child's case.
  (13) The Scottish Ministers may by regulations make provision as to the arrangements mentioned in subsection (11)(b) above.
  (14) Regulations under subsection (13) above may in particular include provision—
    (a) prescribing what method or methods of monitoring compliance with the restriction mentioned in paragraph (a) of subsection (11) above may be specified in a supervision requirement;
    (b) specifying the devices which may be used for the purpose of that monitoring;
    (c) prescribing the person who may be designated by a children's hearing to carry out that monitoring or the class or description of person from which that person may be drawn;
    (d) requiring a children's hearing who have designated a person in pursuance of paragraph (c) above who is no longer within the provision made under that paragraph to vary the designation accordingly and notify the child of the variation.
  (15) The Scottish Ministers may, by contract or otherwise, secure the services of such persons as they think fit to carry out the monitoring mentioned in subsection (11)(b) above and may do so in a way in which those services are provided differently in relation to different areas or different forms of that monitoring.
  (16) Nothing in any enactment or rule of law prevents the disclosure to a person providing services in pursuance of subsection (15) above of information relating to a child where the disclosure is made for the purposes only of the full and proper provision of the monitoring mentioned in subsection (11)(b) above.
  (17) A children's hearing may include in a supervision requirement a movement restriction condition only if the hearing is constituted from the children's panel for a local government area which is prescribed for the purposes of this section by the Scottish Ministers.".

GENERAL NOTE
  At present a children's hearing making a supervision requirement has the power to specify as part of that requirement that child is kept in secure accommodation. Before doing this, however, the hearing must be satisfied that one of two conditions applies to the child, these are set out in the amendment contained in subs.(3). This section gives the hearing the power,

where one of these conditions is satisfied, to impose a movement restriction condition as an alternative to requiring residence in secure accommodation. This condition is essentially the same as a restriction of liberty order and will restrict the movements of the child and require monitoring of his/her movements to ensure compliance with the condition. The reference in the new subs.(12) introduced in subs.(3) of this section is to conditions which are designed to provide intensive support for the child, see Stage 2 debate, Communities Committee, May 26, 2004, Official Report, cols 1168–1169.

Further procedural requirements are contained in The Intensive Support and Monitoring (Scotland) Regulations 2005 (SSI 2005/129) as amended by The Intensive Support and Monitoring (Scotland) Amendment Regulations 2005 (SSI 2005/201). These require the local authority to develop a movement restriction care plan for the child subject to the type of requirement introduced here. Although the original regulations made the existence of such a plan a precondition for the making of a requirement containing a condition restricting movement, this is no longer the case. In addition the local authority must identify someone (not necessarily a local authority employee) to monitor compliance with the conditions contained in the requirement and review compliance with these at least weekly. The regulations also set out the conditions which must form part of the supervision requirement.

Supervision requirements: duties of local authorities

136.—(1) In section 70 of the Children (Scotland) Act 1995 (c. 36) (supervision requirements)—

(a) after subsection (3) there shall be inserted—

"(3A) A children's hearing may, for the purpose of enabling a child to comply with a supervision requirement, impose such duties on the relevant local authority as may be specified in the supervision requirement.

(3B) The duties imposed under subsection (3A) above may include that of securing or facilitating the provision for the child of services of a kind other than that provided by the relevant local authority."; and

(b) after subsection (7) there shall be inserted—

"(7A) Where, on a review under subsection (7) above, it appears to the children's hearing that the relevant local authority are in breach of a duty imposed on them under section 71 of this Act, the hearing may direct the Principal Reporter to give the authority notice of an intended application under section 71A(2) of this Act.

(7B) The Principal Reporter shall, at the same time as giving the notice of an intended application under section 71A(2) of this Act, send a copy of the notice to—

(a) the child to whom the duty referred to in subsection (7A) above relates;

(b) any person who, in relation to the child, is a relevant person;

(c) any person appointed under section 41 of this Act to safeguard the interests of the child in any proceedings which are taking place when the notice is given.

(7C) Notice of an intended application under section 71A(2) of this Act is a written notice—

(a) setting out the respects in which the relevant local authority are in breach of the duty imposed on them under section 71 of this Act; and

(b) stating that if the authority do not comply with that duty within the period of 21 days beginning with the day on which they received the notice, the Principal Reporter may make an application under section 71A(2) of this Act.

(7D) Where a children's hearing have made a direction under subsection (7A) above, they shall determine that a further review under subsection (7) above take place on or as soon as is reasonably practicable after the expiry of the period of 28 days beginning with the day on which notice was given in pursuance of that direction.

(7E) Where on a further review under subsection (7) above which takes place by virtue of subsection (7D) above, it appears to the children's hearing that the relevant local authority continues to be in breach of the duty referred to in subsection (7A) above, the hearing may authorise the Principal Reporter to make an application under section 71A(2) of this Act.".

(2) In section 71 of that Act (duties of local authority with respect to supervision requirements), after subsection (1) there shall be inserted—
"(1A) Where a supervision requirement imposes, under section 70(3A) of this Act, duties on the relevant local authority, the authority shall perform those duties.".

(3) After that section, there shall be inserted—

"Enforcement of local authorities' duties under section 71

71A.—(1) The sheriff principal may, on an application under subsection (2) below, make an order requiring a relevant local authority in breach of a duty imposed on them under section 71 of this Act to perform that duty.

(2) The Principal Reporter, having been so authorised by a children's hearing under section 70(7E) of this Act, may apply for an order under subsection (1) above.

(3) No such application shall be competent unless—

(a) the Principal Reporter has, on a direction of the children's hearing made under section 70(7A) of this Act, given the relevant local authority the notice referred to in that provision; and

(b) the authority have failed to comply, within the period stipulated in the notice, with the duty there referred to.

(4) In deciding whether to apply under subsection (2) above, the Principal Reporter shall not take into account any factor relating to the adequacy of the means available to the relevant local authority to enable it to comply with the duty.

(5) An application under subsection (2) above shall be made by summary application.

(6) The sheriff principal having jurisdiction under this section is the sheriff principal of the sheriffdom in which is situated the principal office of the relevant local authority in breach of the duty referred to in subsection (1) above.

(7) An order under subsection (1) above shall be final.".

GENERAL NOTE

Although s.71 of the Children (Scotland) Act 1995 imposes a duty on local authorities to give effect to the requirements of a supervision requirement, there was no formal mechanism for making sure that this happened and also considerable evidence that supervision requirements wee not being supervised and implemented (for example, Audit Scotland, *Dealing with offending by young people*, (2002), paras 147–148). The provisions introduced by this section into the Children (Scotland) Act 1995 are designed to provide a process by which both duties imposed on a local authority by a supervision requirement can be clearly specified and these duties can be enforced in the event of non-compliance.

Where duties on the local authority are clearly identified and there are concerns that these may not be fulfilled it may be appropriate for the hearing to exercise its power to set a review date so that the compliance of the authority with the requirement can be monitored. In any event, where at a review of a supervision requirement it appears that the authority is in breach of a duty imposed on them the hearing can direct the Reporter to give the local authority notice of an intention to apply to the sheriff principal for an order requiring the authority to perform the duty. The hearing has discretion on whether to direct the service of the notice.

The draft guidance suggests that a requirement should only be made where there is a specific failure that, if left unchecked, would have a serious impact on the young person (Scottish Executive, *Guidance on Local Authority Accountability*, February 2005, para.43). The notice gives the authority 21 days to respond. After this period has passed the hearing will meet again to consider the response and decide whether to authorise the Reporter to apply for an enforcement order. Once authorised, the Reporter then has to decide whether to make the application. In taking this decision any lack of resources on the part of the authority must not be taken into account. The application is made direct to the sheriff principal who has the power to order to authority to perform their duty.

Despite the confidence expressed in the *Guidance* that progress is being made to tackle the lack of resources which underlies the difficulties which many authorities have in fulfilling their responsibilities statistics published shortly after the Act came into effect show average vacancies for social workers running at 13% for children's services, with overall vacancy rates for individual authorities running as high as 37% (Social Worker Posts And Vacancies: October 2004, November 8, 2004, these figures had reduced to 12 per cent and 31 per cent by April 2005, *Social Work Posts and Vacancies: April 2005*, available at: http://www.scotland.gov.uk/Publications/2005/06/22113343/33452).

Failure to provide education for excluded pupils

Failure to provide education for excluded pupils: reference

137.—(1) The Children (Scotland) Act 1995 (c.36) shall be amended as follows.

(2) In subsection (4) of section 56 (steps where no reference to children's hearing)—

  (a) the word "and" where it occurs immediately after paragraph (a) shall be repealed; and

  (b) after paragraph (b) there shall be inserted
"; and

  (c) he may, where it appears to him that—

    (i) an education authority have a duty under section 14(3) of the Education (Scotland) Act 1980 (c.44) in relation to the child; and

    (ii) the authority are not complying with that duty,
refer the matter to the Scottish Ministers.

(4A) A reference made under subsection (4)(c) above shall be in writing.

(4B) A copy of a reference made under subsection (4)(c) above shall be sent by the Principal Reporter to the education authority in respect of which the reference is made.".

(3) After section 75 there shall be inserted—

"Failure to provide education for excluded pupils

Failure to provide education for excluded pupils: reference to Scottish Ministers

75B.—(1) Where it appears to the children's hearing to whom a child's case has been referred under section 65(1) of this Act that—

  (a) an education authority have a duty under section 14(3) of the Education (Scotland) Act 1980 (c.44) in relation to the child; and

  (b) the authority are not complying with that duty,
they may require the Principal Reporter to refer the matter to the Scottish Ministers.

(2) The Principal Reporter shall comply with any requirement made under subsection (1) above.

(3) A reference made by virtue of subsection (1) above shall be in writing.

(4) A copy of a reference made by virtue of subsection (1) above shall be sent by the Principal Reporter to the education authority in respect of which the reference is made.".

(4) In subsection (1) of section 93 (interpretation of Part II), after the definition of "disabled" there shall be inserted—

""education authority" has the meaning given by section 135(1) of the Education (Scotland) Act 1980 (c.44);".

GENERAL NOTE

These amendments to the Children (Scotland) Act 1995 are designed to give additional powers to the Reporter and to children's hearings in cases where a child has been excluded from school and where the local authority does not appear to be complying with its obligation to provide alternative education to that child. The power is to report the case to the Scottish Ministers who have enforcement powers in relation to local authority discharge of their education function.

PART 13

MISCELLANEOUS AND GENERAL

Miscellaneous

Privacy of certain proceedings

138.—(1) Subject to subsection (2)—

(a) proceedings mentioned in subsection (4) shall be conducted and determined in private; and

(b) no person other than a person whose presence is necessary for their proper consideration shall be present.

(2) The court before which particular proceedings are taking place may direct that the proceedings—

(a) shall take place in public; or

(b) shall take place in the presence of such additional persons as the court may direct.

(3) A direction under subsection (2) may be given in respect of the whole, or any part, of proceedings.

(4) The proceedings referred to in subsection (1) are—

(a) proceedings before a sheriff on an application for—

    (i) an order under section 4(1) in respect of a child;

    (ii) the variation, or revocation, under section 5(1) of such an order;

    (iii) an order under section 102(1); or

    (iv) the variation, or revocation, under section 105(1) of an order made under section 13(1) or 102(1);

(b) proceedings before a sheriff for the purpose of considering whether—

    (i) to make an order under section 7(2) in respect of a child;

    (ii) to recall such an order;

    (iii) to make a requirement under section 12(1);

    (iv) to make an order under section 13(1); or

    (v) to make an order under section 105(5); and

(c) an appeal arising from proceedings mentioned in paragraph (a) or (b).

GENERAL NOTE

Subject to the power of the court under subs.(2) to direct that proceedings take place in public or that additional persons are allowed to be present, this section provides that the proceedings set out in subs.(4) are to take place in private.

Disclosure and sharing of information

139.—(1) Where subsection (2) applies, any person who, apart from this subsection—

(a) would not have power to disclose information to a relevant authority; or

(b) would be by virtue of any enactment (including subsection (3)) or rule of law susceptible to a sanction or other remedy if the person disclosed the information,

shall have that power or shall not be susceptible to that sanction or remedy.

(2) This subsection applies if the disclosure is necessary or expedient for the purposes of any provision of—

(a) this Act; or

(b) any other enactment the purpose of which is to make provision for or in connection with antisocial behaviour or its effects.

(3) Subject to subsection (4), where—

(a) by virtue of subsection (1) a person discloses to a relevant authority information in respect of which the person is subject to a duty of confidentiality; and

(b) on disclosing the information, the person informs the authority of the breach of the duty,

the authority shall not disclose the information.

(4) Subsection (3) shall not prevent disclosure in any case where disclosure is permitted or required by virtue of any enactment or rule of law.

(5) In subsections (1) and (3), "relevant authority" means—

(a) a local authority;

(b) a chief constable;

(c) the Principal Reporter;

(d) a registered social landlord;

(e) an authority administering housing benefit;

(f) a person providing services relating to housing benefit to, or authorised to discharge any function relating to housing benefit of—

   (i) a local authority; or

   (ii) an authority administering housing benefit.

(6) Any person who, by virtue of this Act, must or may provide information or who provides or receives information for the purposes of any provision of this Act shall have regard to any relevant guidance given by the Scottish Ministers.

(7) The Scottish Ministers may, by order, modify the meaning of "relevant authority" in subsection (5).

DEFINITIONS
"relevant authority":   subs.(5)

GENERAL NOTE

This section is designed to facilitate the exchange of information where this exchange is connected with tackling antisocial behaviour. There are two main provisions, the first of these is a power to disclose information where disclosure is necessary or expedient for the purposes of any statutory provision concerned with antisocial behaviour. This extends the scope beyond this Act, for example to allow disclosure to a registered social landlord considering eviction on the grounds of antisocial behaviour under the Housing (Scotland) Act 2001. The second provision restricts further disclosure where the initial discloser makes it clear that they are acting in breach of confidence. Even where this is done, however, further disclosure of this information may still take place by virtue of subs.(5). It is not perhaps entirely clear what this section adds, for example, to the normal rules of breach of confidence which permit such a breach when there is a public interest in information being disclosed. Reference should also be made to Scottish Executive, *Guidance on Disclosure and Sharing of Information*, October 2004.

Equal opportunities

140.—(1) Any person discharging a function by virtue of this Act shall discharge that function in a manner that encourages equal opportunities and in particular the observance of the equal opportunity requirements.

(2) In subsection (1), "equal opportunities" and "equal opportunity requirements" have the same meanings as in Section L2 of Part II of Schedule 5 to the Scotland Act 1998 (c.46).

GENERAL NOTE

In the Crime and Disorder Act 1998 these terms are defined as follows:

"Equal opportunities" means the prevention, elimination or regulation of discrimination between persons on grounds of sex or marital status, on racial grounds, or on grounds of disability, age, sexual orientation, language or social origin, or of other personal attributes, including beliefs or opinions, such as religious beliefs or political opinions.

"Equal opportunity requirements" means the requirements of the law for the time being relating to equal opportunities.

General

Orders and regulations

141.—(1) Any power conferred by this Act on the Scottish Ministers to make orders or regulations shall be exercisable by statutory instrument.

(2) Any power conferred by this Act on the Scottish Ministers to make orders or regulations—

(a) may be exercised so as to make different provision for different cases or descriptions of case or for different purposes; and

(b) includes power to make such incidental, supplementary, consequential, transitory, transitional or saving provision as the Scottish Ministers consider appropriate.

(3) A statutory instrument containing an order or regulations made under this Act (other than an order under section 145(2)) shall, subject to subsection (4), be subject to annulment in pursuance of a resolution of the Scottish Parliament.

(4) A statutory instrument containing—

(a) an order under section 53(1), 59(1), 68(6), 83(7), 103(3), 128(2) or 139(7); or

(b) regulations under section 26(2),

shall not be made unless a draft of the instrument has been laid before, and approved by resolution of, the Scottish Parliament.

Directions

142.—(1) Any power conferred by virtue of this Act on the Scottish Ministers to give a direction shall include power to vary or revoke the direction.

(2) Any direction given by virtue of this Act by the Scottish Ministers shall be in writing.

Interpretation: "antisocial behaviour" and other expressions

143.—(1) For the purposes of this Act (other than Parts 7 and 8), a person ("A") engages in antisocial behaviour if A—

(a) acts in a manner that causes or is likely to cause alarm or distress; or

112

   (b) pursues a course of conduct that causes or is likely to cause alarm or distress,

      to at least one person who is not of the same household as A; and "antisocial behaviour" shall be construed accordingly.

   (2) In this Act, unless the context otherwise requires—

      "conduct" includes speech; and a course of conduct must involve conduct on at least two occasions;

      "local authority" means a council constituted under section 2 of the Local Government etc. (Scotland) Act 1994 (c.39); and "area", in relation to a local authority, means the local government area (within the meaning of that Act) for which the council is constituted;

      "registered social landlord" means a body registered in the register maintained under section 57 of the Housing (Scotland) Act 2001 (asp 10); and

      "senior police officer" has the meaning given by section 19(1).

GENERAL NOTE

    There are a number of points to note about the definition of antisocial behaviour. First, it must be behaviour that causes or is likely to cause alarm or distress. This may not be a high threshold given the historical approach of the court in Scotland to defining Breach of the Peace, a crime which can involve behaviour likely to cause alarm and distress. In some cases the threshold has been set at a low level (see the discussion, for example, in Christie, S, *Introduction to Scottish Criminal* Law, 175–180). More recently the definition has been strengthened in *Smith v Donnelly*, 2001 S.L.T. 1007. The discussion in *Smith* focussed on whether breach of the peace was defined with sufficient clarity to meet the requirement for certainty in criminal offences set out in Art.7 of the European Convention on Human Rights. It was held that it was, and in the process the offence was defined as involving conduct which was, in its context, genuinely alarming and disturbing to any reasonable person. It was also pointed out that where there was no evidence of actual alarm, the conduct of the defendant must be flagrant in order to justify a conviction. This arguably sets a higher standard than some older cases (see Jones T & Christie M, *Criminal Law* (3rd ed.), 12–11—12–15). Although in most cases the decision as to whether behaviour is antisocial will be taken in a civil rather than a criminal court the infringement of Convention rights which can follow from an ASBO or other order based on this behaviour suggests that a standard similar to that applied now in cases of Breach of the Peace should be used.

    Secondly, the distress/alarm must be caused to someone outside the household of the person who is behaving in an antisocial manner. Finally, and perhaps most importantly, there is no reference to the cause of the behaviour and no reference to an intention to cause alarm or distress. The net is potentially drawn very wide to include those with either limited or no control over their behaviours, for example those with Tourette's syndrome, those who may not realise or understand the consequences of their action (for example those with an autistic spectrum disorder) and those who may not be able to form any sort of intention (for example those suffering from serious mental illness or from severe learning difficulties). Despite the arguable undesirability of dealing with these groups by way of an ASBO the matter is deal with largely through guidance (see General Note to s.4) rather than by specific provision in the Act, though an attempt was made to do this while the Act was being passed. In practice the requirement that an ASBO is necessary to prevent future antic social behaviour (see s.4) should cut out many of these cases, as where there is no intention, understanding or control an ASBO will not have an effect on future conduct. Despite this, there is some evidence of orders being used inappropriately in England and Wales (referred to, for example in the evidence of the National Autistic Society to the Communities Committee at Stage 1, Official Report, January 14, 2004, cols 429–452).

    Where alarm or distress is caused by the actions of a number of individuals, though might not be caused by one person acting alone, the possibility of individual behaviour satisfying the criteria for antisocial behaviour is considered in *Chief Constable of Lancashire v Potter* [2003] EWHC 2272 (Admin). In *Moat Housing Group Ltd v Harris & Anr* [2005] EWCA Civ 287 the question was raised but not considered of whether a failure to control ones children amounts to an act for the purposes of the definition of anti-social behaviour (para.167).

Minor and consequential amendments and repeals

   144.—(1) Schedule 4 (which contains minor amendments and amendments consequential on the provisions of this Act) shall have effect.

(2) The enactments mentioned in the first column in schedule 5 (which include enactments that are spent) are repealed to the extent set out in the second column.

Short title and commencement

145.—(1) This Act may be cited as the Antisocial Behaviour etc. (Scotland) Act 2004.

(2) This Act (other than this section and section 141) shall come into force on such day as the Scottish Ministers may by order appoint.

SCHEDULE 1

(introduced by section 47(9))

POWERS IN RELATION TO EQUIPMENT SEIZED UNDER SECTION 47

Interpretation

1 In this schedule—
   (a) "noise offence" means, in relation to equipment seized under section 47(2), an offence under section 45;
   (b) "seized equipment" means equipment seized in the exercise of the power of seizure and removal conferred by section 47(2);
   (c) "related equipment", in relation to any conviction of, or proceedings for a noise offence, means seized equipment used or alleged to have been used in the commission of the offence;
   (d) "responsible local authority", in relation to seized equipment, means the local authority by or on whose behalf the equipment was seized.

Retention

2 (1) Any seized equipment may be retained—
   (a) during the period of 28 days beginning with the seizure; or
   (b) if it is related equipment in proceedings for a noise offence instituted within that period against any person, until—
      (i) that person is sentenced or otherwise dealt with for, or acquitted of, the offence; or
      (ii) the proceedings are discontinued.
   (2) Sub-paragraph (1) does not authorise the retention of seized equipment if—
   (a) a person has been given a fixed penalty notice under section 46 in respect of any noise;
   (b) the equipment was seized because of its use in the emission of the noise in respect of which the fixed penalty notice was given; and
   (c) that person has paid the fixed penalty before the end of the period allowed for its payment.

Forfeiture

3 (1) Where a person is convicted of a noise offence the court may make an order (a "forfeiture order") for forfeiture of any related equipment.
   (2) The court may make a forfeiture order whether or not it deals also with the offender in respect of the offence in any other way and without regard to any restrictions on forfeiture in any enactment.
   (3) In considering whether to make a forfeiture order in respect of any equipment, a court shall have regard—
   (a) to the value of the equipment; and
   (b) to the likely financial and other effects on the offender of the making of the order (taken with any other order that the court contemplates making).
   (4) A forfeiture order operates to deprive the offender of any rights in the equipment to which it relates.

Consequences of forfeiture

4 (1) Where any equipment has been forfeited under paragraph 3, the sheriff may, on the application of a person (other than the person in whose case the forfeiture order was made) who claims the equipment, make an order for delivery of the equipment to the applicant.
   (2) An order such as is mentioned in sub-paragraph (1) may only be made if the sheriff is satisfied that the applicant is the owner of the equipment.
   (3) No application may be made under sub-paragraph (1) after the expiry of the period of 6 months beginning with the date on which a forfeiture order was made in respect of the equipment.
   (4) Where the responsible local authority is of the opinion that the person in whose case the forfeiture order was made is not the owner of the equipment, it must take reasonable steps to

115

bring to the attention of persons who may be entitled to do so their right to make an application under sub-paragraph (1).

(5) An order under sub-paragraph (1) does not affect the right of any person to take, within the period of 6 months beginning with the date of the order, proceedings for the recovery of the equipment from the person in possession of it in pursuance of the order (but the right ceases on the expiry of that period).

(6) If, on the expiry of the period of 6 months beginning with the date on which a forfeiture order was made in respect of the equipment, no order has been made under sub-paragraph (1), the responsible local authority may dispose of the equipment.

Return etc. of seized equipment

5 If in proceedings for a noise offence no order for forfeiture of related equipment is made, the court may (whether or not a person is convicted of the offence) give such directions as it thinks fit as to the return, retention or disposal of the equipment by the responsible local authority.

6 (1) Where in the case of any seized equipment no proceedings in which it is related equipment are begun within the period mentioned in paragraph 2(1)(a)—

    (a) the responsible local authority shall return the equipment to any person who—
        (i) appears to it to be the owner of the equipment; and
        (ii) makes a claim for the return of the equipment within the period mentioned in sub-paragraph (2); and
    (b) if no such person makes such a claim within that period, the responsible local authority may dispose of the equipment.

(2) The period referred to in sub-paragraph (1)(a)(ii) is the period of 6 months beginning with the expiry of the period mentioned in paragraph 2(1)(a).

(3) The responsible local authority shall take reasonable steps to bring to the attention of persons who may be entitled to do so their right to make such a claim.

(4) Subject to sub-paragraph (6), the responsible local authority is not required to return any seized equipment under sub-paragraph (1)(a) until the person making the claim has paid any such reasonable charges for the seizure, removal and retention of the equipment as the authority may demand.

(5) If—
    (a) equipment is sold in pursuance of—
        (i) paragraph 4(6);
        (ii) directions under paragraph 5; or
        (iii) this paragraph; and
    (b) before the expiration of the period of one year beginning with the date on which the equipment is sold any person satisfies the responsible local authority that at the time of its sale the person was the owner of the equipment,
the authority shall pay that person any sum by which any proceeds of sale exceed any such reasonable charges for the seizure, removal or retention of the equipment as the authority may demand.

(6) The responsible local authority cannot demand charges from any person under sub-paragraph (4) or (5) who it is satisfied did not know, and had no reason to suspect, that the equipment was likely to be used in the emission of noise exceeding the level determined under section 48.

SCHEDULE 2

(introduced by section 66)

PENALTIES FOR CERTAIN ENVIRONMENTAL OFFENCES

PART 1

ACTS

The Sewerage (Scotland) Act 1968 (c.47)

1 (1) The Sewerage (Scotland) Act 1968 shall be amended as follows.
(2) In section 12(8) (connection with public sewers), for "£20,000" substitute "£40,000".

(3) In section 24(2) (discharge into public sewers), for "£20,000" substitute "£40,000".

(4) In section 46(2) (injurious matter in sewers), for "£20,000" substitute "£40,000".

The Control of Pollution Act 1974 (c.40)

2 (1) The Control of Pollution Act 1974 shall be amended as follows.

(2) In section 30F(6) (pollution offences), in paragraph (a), for "£20,000" substitute "£40,000".

(3) In section 46D(2) (non-compliance with a works notice), in paragraph (a), for "£20,000" substitute "£40,000".

(4) In section 49A(3) (non-compliance with an enforcement notice), in paragraph (a), for "£20,000" substitute "£40,000".

The Water (Scotland) Act 1980 (c.45)

3 Section 75 of the Water (Scotland) Act 1980 (penalty for polluting water) shall be amended as follows—

(a)   in subsection (3), in paragraph (a), for "the prescribed sum" substitute "£40,000"; and

(b)   subsection (4) is repealed.

The Environmental Protection Act 1990 (c.43)

4 (1) The 1990 Act shall be amended as follows.

(2) In section 23(2) (offences under Part 1), in paragraph (a), for "£20,000" substitute "£40,000".

(3) In section 33 (prohibition on disposal of waste), in—

(a)   subsection (8), in paragraph (a); and

(b)   subsection (9), in paragraph (a),

for "£20,000" substitute "£40,000".

(4) In section 80(6) (contravention of an abatement notice), for "£20,000" substitute "£40,000".

The Pollution Prevention and Control Act 1999 (c.24)

5 In paragraph 25(2)(a)(ii) of Schedule 1 to the Pollution Prevention and Control Act 1999 (offences), for "£20,000" substitute "£40,000".

The Water Environment and Water Services (Scotland) Act 2003 (asp 3)

6 In paragraph 20(2)(a)(ii) of schedule 2 to the Water Environment and Water Services (Scotland) Act 2003 (offences), for "£20,000" substitute "£40,000".

PART 2

SUBORDINATE LEGISLATION

The Pollution Prevention and Control (Scotland) Regulations 2000 (S.S.I. 2000/323)

7 In paragraph (2)(a) of regulation 30 of the Pollution Prevention and Control (Scotland) Regulations 2000 (offences), for "£20,000" substitute "£40,000".

The Landfill (Scotland) Regulations 2003 (S.S.I. 2003/235)

8 In paragraph (2)(a) of regulation 19 of the Landfill (Scotland) Regulations 2003 (offences), for "£20,000" substitute "£40,000".

SCHEDULE 3

(introduced by section 74(5))

MANAGEMENT CONTROL ORDERS

Application and interpretation

1 (1) Paragraphs 2 to 6 apply while an order is in force in respect of a house.
(2) In this schedule—
"management period", in relation to an order, means the period specified in the order; and
"order" means a management control order.

Effect of order

2 The order shall not affect the rights or liabilities of any person who, at the time when the order is made, is occupying the relevant house under the tenancy or, as the case may be, occupancy arrangement.

Accounts

3 (1) The local authority shall pay to such relevant person as it considers appropriate—
  (a) any surplus of its income over its expenditure in respect of the house to which the order relates; and
  (b) the interest on any such surplus at such reasonable rate as the authority may determine.
(2) The local authority shall—
  (a) keep accounts for the management period of its income and expenditure in respect of the house to which the order relates; and
  (b) afford to the relevant person all reasonable facilities for inspecting, taking copies of and verifying those accounts.
(3) The Scottish Ministers may by regulations make provision about—
  (a) expenditure which local authorities may incur in respect of houses to which orders relate; and
  (b) the means of recovering such expenditure.
(4) For the purposes of this paragraph "relevant person" means the person who, immediately before the order was made, was the landlord of the house to which the order relates.

Recovery of rent arrears etc.

4 If during the management period—
  (a) rent payable; or
  (b) consideration payable or exigible,
    under the tenancy or occupancy arrangement is not paid or made, the authority shall take all reasonable steps to recover the rent or consideration.

Delegation of management functions

5 The local authority may authorise any person to do in relation to the relevant house anything that the authority is, by virtue of the order, entitled to do.

New tenancies and occupancy arrangements

6 (1) Where—
  (a) the house to which an order relates is occupied by virtue of—
      (i) two or more tenancies;
      (ii) two or more occupancy arrangements; or
      (iii) one or more tenancies and one or more occupancy arrangements; and
  (b) during the management period, one of those tenancies or occupancy arrangements (the "old occupancy right") ends,

118

the person who, immediately before the order was made, was the landlord of the house may, if the local authority agrees, grant a tenancy or make an occupancy arrangement in respect of the part of the house that was subject to the old occupancy right.

(2) Any rights and obligations of the landlord under a tenancy granted, or an occupancy arrangement made, by virtue of sub-paragraph (1) shall be deemed to have been transferred, by virtue of the order relating to the house, to the local authority specified in the order.

SCHEDULE 4

(introduced by section 144(1))

MINOR AND CONSEQUENTIAL AMENDMENTS

The Social Work (Scotland) Act 1968 (c.49)

1 In section 27 of the Social Work (Scotland) Act 1968 (functions of local authorities in relation to persons appearing before courts, under supervision of court orders etc.)—
   (a) in subsection (1)—
      (i) after paragraph (ac) insert—
        "(ad) making available, for the purposes of parenting orders under section 13 or 102 of the Antisocial Behaviour etc. (Scotland) Act 2004 (asp 8), such services as are required to enable requirements imposed by or under such orders to be carried out in respect of persons in their area;"; and
      (ii) in paragraph (b), after sub-paragraph (v) insert—
        "(va) without prejudice to sub-paragraph (i) above, persons in their area who are subject to community reparation orders under section 245K of the said Act of 1995;
        (vb) without prejudice to sub-paragraph (i) above, persons in their area who are under 16 years of age and subject to restriction of liberty orders under section 245A of the said Act of 1995;";
   (b) in each of subsections (2) to (5), for the words "probation, community service and supervised attendance", wherever they occur, substitute "community justice"; and
   (c) after subsection (5) insert—
      "(5A) Before including in a community justice scheme which is made, revised or modified under this section provision for the purposes of subsection (1)(b)(va), a local authority shall consult such persons or class or classes of person as the Scottish Ministers may by regulations prescribe.
      (5B) The Scottish Ministers may give local authorities directions in writing as to the content of community justice schemes; and authorities shall comply with any such directions.
      (5C) The power conferred by subsection (5B) above to give a direction shall include power to vary or revoke the direction.".

The Housing (Scotland) Act 1987 (c.26)

2 In subsection (2C)(c) of section 31 of the Housing (Scotland) Act 1987 (duties to persons found to be homeless), for "anti-social behaviour order under section 19 of the Crime and Disorder Act 1998 (c.37)" there shall be substituted "antisocial behaviour order—
   (i) under section 234AA of the Criminal Procedure (Scotland) Act 1995 (c.46); or
   (ii) under section 4 of the Antisocial Behaviour etc. (Scotland) Act 2004 (asp 8)".

The Environmental Protection Act 1990 (c.43)

3 After section 81(3) of the Environmental Protection Act 1990 (power to abate statutory nuisance) there shall be inserted—
"(3A) The power under subsection (3) above shall, where the matter to be abated is a statutory nuisance by virtue of section 79(1)(g) above, include power to seize and remove any equipment which it appears to the authority is being or has been used in the emission of the noise in question.

(3B) A person who wilfully obstructs any person exercising, by virtue of subsection (3A) above, the power conferred by subsection (3) above shall be liable, on summary conviction, to a fine not exceeding level 3 on the standard scale.

(3C) Schedule 1 to the Antisocial Behaviour etc. (Scotland) Act 2004 (asp 8) shall have effect in relation to equipment seized by virtue of subsection (3A) above as it does in relation to equipment seized under section 47(2) of that Act, subject to the following modifications—

    (a) in paragraph 1(a), "noise offence" means an offence under section 80(4) above in respect of a statutory nuisance falling within section 79(1)(g) above; and

    (b) in paragraph 1(b), "seized equipment" means equipment seized by virtue of subsection (3A) above.".

The Children (Scotland) Act 1995 (c.36)

4 (1) The Children (Scotland) Act 1995 shall be amended as follows.

(2) In section 51(5) (powers of sheriff on allowing appeal against decision of children's hearing), in paragraph (b) for the words from "condition" to "70(9)" substitute "movement restriction condition imposed under subsection (3)(b) of section 70 of this Act or a condition imposed under subsection (9) of that section".

(3) In subsection (6) of section 66 (warrant to keep child where hearing unable to dispose of case), for the words from "that", where it first occurs, to "satisfied" substitute—

    "(a) that one of the conditions mentioned in section 70(10) of this Act is met; and

    (b) that it is necessary to do so,".

(4) In subsection (11) of section 68 (application to sheriff to establish grounds of referral), for the words from "that", where it first occurs, to "fulfilled" substitute—

    "(a) that one of the conditions mentioned in section 70(10) of this Act is met; and

    (b) that it is necessary for the order to do so,".

(5) In subsection (11) of section 69 (continuation or disposal of referral by children's hearing) for the words from "that", where it first occurs, to "fulfilled" substitute—

    "(a) that one of the conditions mentioned in section 70(10) of this Act is met; and

    (b) that it is necessary to do so,".

(6) In section 93 (interpretation of Part 2)—

    (a) in subsection (1), in the definition of "relevant local authority"—

        (i) after "area" insert "there is established"; and

        (ii) for "formed" substitute "constituted"; and

    (b) in subsection (2), in paragraph (b), after "3" insert "(except section 75A)".

The Criminal Procedure (Scotland) Act 1995 (c.46)

5 (1) The Criminal Procedure (Scotland) Act 1995 shall be amended as follows.

(2) In subsection (2)(b)(ii) of section 79 (preliminary pleas and preliminary issues), after "Act" there shall be inserted "section 9(6) of the Antisocial Behaviour etc. (Scotland) Act 2004 (asp 8) or that section of that Act as applied by section 234AA(11) of this Act".

(3) In subsection (4) of section 193A (suspension of certain sentences pending determination of appeal), after paragraph (d) there shall be inserted—

    "(e) a community reparation order.".

(4) In section 219 (imprisonment for non-payment of fines)—

    (a) in subsection (1), after "Act" there shall be inserted "and subsection (1A) below"; and

    (b) after subsection (1) there shall be inserted—

        "(1A) Subsection (1) shall not apply to a fine imposed for an offence under section 107 of the Antisocial Behaviour etc. (Scotland) Act 2004 (asp 8).".

(5) In section 235 (supervised attendance orders)—

    (a) in subsection (1), after "(4)" there shall be inserted "or (4A)";

    (b) after subsection (2), there shall be inserted—

        "(2A) In making a supervised attendance order where subsection (4A) below applies, a court shall take into consideration the best interests of any person under the age of 16 in respect of whom the offender has parental responsibilities within the meaning of Part I of the Children (Scotland) Act 1995 (c.36).";

    (c) after subsection (4), there shall be inserted—

"(4A) This subsection applies where, having been convicted of an offence under section 107 of the Antisocial Behaviour etc. (Scotland) Act 2004 (asp 8), the offender has had imposed on him a fine which (or any part or instalment of which) he has failed to pay."; and

  (d) in subsection (6)—

      (i) the word "or", where it first appears, is omitted; and

     (ii) after "(4)(c)" there shall be inserted "or (4A)".

(6) In subsection (3) of section 239 (requirements of community service orders), after "works" there shall be inserted "(or carries out voluntary work)".

(7) In section 245D (combination of restriction of liberty order with probation order or drug treatment and testing order)—

  (a) in subsection (1)(b)—

      (i) after "to", where it first occurs, there shall be inserted—

"(i) in the case of an offender who is under 16 years of age,";

     (ii) for "or to", where those words first occur, there shall be substituted—

"(ii) in the case of an offender who is 16 years of age or more, a probation order made under section 228(1) of this Act,"; and

    (iii) the word "to", where it thirdly occurs, is repealed; and

  (b) in subsection (3), after "and", where it secondly occurs, there shall be inserted—

"(a) in the case of an offender who is under 16 years of age, a probation order;

(b) in the case of an offender who is 16 years of age or more,".

(8) In subsection (1)(b) of section 245E (variation of restriction of liberty orders), after "court,", where it first occurs, there shall be inserted "apply".

(9) In subsection (2) of section 245G (disposal on revocation of restriction of liberty order), after "disposing" there shall be inserted "of".

(10) In subsection (1)(b) of section 245H (documentary evidence in proceedings under section 245F), for "person subject to the order" there shall be substituted "offender".

(11) In paragraph 3 of Schedule 7 (supervised attendance orders)—

  (a) in sub-paragraph (1), after "works" there shall be inserted "(or carries out voluntary work)"; and

  (b) in sub-paragraph (3), after "works" there shall be inserted "(or carries out voluntary work)".

(12) In Schedule 9 (certificates as to proof of certain routine matters), at the end there shall be inserted the following entry—

The Antisocial Behaviour etc. (Scotland) Act 2004 (asp 8), section 45(1).	An officer of a local authority within the meaning of that Act authorised to do so by the authority.	That a level of noise specified in the certificate was measured at a time and in a place specified in the certificate using an approved device within the meaning of that Act.

The Housing (Scotland) Act 2001 (asp 10)

6 (1) The Housing (Scotland) Act 2001 shall be amended as follows.

(2) In section 35(2) (conversion to short Scottish secure tenancy), for "anti-social behaviour order under section 19 of the Crime and Disorder Act 1998 (c.37)" there shall be substituted "antisocial behaviour order—

  (a) under section 234AA of the Criminal Procedure (Scotland) Act 1995 (c.46); or

  (b) under section 4 of the Antisocial Behaviour etc. (Scotland) Act 2004 (asp 8)".

(3) In paragraph 2 of schedule 6 (grounds for granting short Scottish secure tenancy), for "anti-social behaviour order under section 19 of the Crime and Disorder Act 1998 (c.37)" there shall be substituted "antisocial behaviour order—

  (a) under section 234AA of the Criminal Procedure (Scotland) Act 1995 (c.46); or

  (b) under section 4 of the Antisocial Behaviour etc. (Scotland) Act 2004 (asp 8)".

SCHEDULE 5

(introduced by section 144(2))

REPEALS

Enactment	Extent of repeal
The Social Work (Scotland) Act 1968 (c.49)	In section 27(2), the words from ", after" to "area,".
The Law Reform (Miscellaneous Provisions) (Scotland) Act 1990 (c.40)	In Schedule 6, paragraph 8(b).
The Criminal Procedure (Consequential Provisions) (Scotland) Act 1995 (c.40)	In Schedule 4, paragraph 30.
The Criminal Procedure (Scotland) Act 1995 (c.46)	In section 245A(1), the words from "and", where it first occurs, to the end.
The Crime and Disorder Act 1998 (c.37)	Section 19. Sections 21, 22 and 22A.
The Criminal Justice (Scotland) Act 2003 (asp 7)	Sections 44 and 45.Section 83.

PART B

SELECTED RELEVANT SCOTTISH STATUTORY INSTRUMENTS

ACT OF SEDERUNT (SUMMARY APPLICATIONS, STATUTORY APPLICATIONS AND APPEALS ETC. RULES) AMENDMENT (ANTI-SOCIAL BEHAVIOUR ETC. (SCOTLAND) ACT 2004) 2004

(SSI 2004/455)

Made   *21st October 2004*
Coming into force in accordance with article 1(1)(b) and (2)

The Lords of Council and Session, under and by virtue of the powers conferred by section 32 of the Sheriff Courts (Scotland) Act 1971, section 27(5)(e) of the Antisocial Behaviour etc. (Scotland) Act 2004, and of all other powers enabling them in that behalf, having approved draft rules submitted to them by the Sheriff Court Rules Council in accordance with section 34 of the said Act of 1971, do hereby enact and declare:

Citation and commencement

1.—(1) This Act of Sederunt—
  (a) may be cited as the Act of Sederunt (Summary Applications, Statutory Applications and Appeals etc. Rules) Amendment (Antisocial Behaviour etc. (Scotland) Act 2004) 2004; (b) shall, subject to the provisions of article 1(2), come into force on 28th October 2004; and(c) shall be inserted in the Books of Sederunt.

(2) In Part XXVII of Chapter 3 of the Act of Sederunt (Summary Applications, Statutory Applications and Appeals etc.) Rules 1999 which is inserted by article 2(4)—
  (a) Rule 3.27.18 shall come into force on 31st January 2005;(b) Rules 3.27.5 and 3.27.15 to 3.27.17 shall come into force on 4th April 2005; and(c) Rules 3.27.12 to 3.27.14 shall come into force on 15th November 2005.

Amendment, revocation and saving of the Summary Application Rules

2.—(1) In the Act of Sederunt (Summary Applications, Statutory Applications and Appeals etc. Rules) 1999, Chapter 3 (rules on applications under specific statutes) is amended in accordance with the following paragraphs.

(2) Part XXII (Crime and Disorder Act 1998) is hereby revoked.

(3) Notwithstanding the revocation of Part XXII by article 2(2), the provisions of Part XXII shall continue in force in relation to applications for an antisocial behaviour order under section 19(3) of the Crime and Disorder Act 1998 commenced before the date of that revocation.

(4) After Part XXVI (Protection of Children (Scotland) Act 2003) insert—

"PART XXVII
ANTISOCIAL BEHAVIOUR ETC. (SCOTLAND) ACT 2004

Interpretation
3.27.1.—(1) In this Part—

"the Act" means the Antisocial Behaviour etc. (Scotland) Act 2004;
"ASBO" means an antisocial behaviour order under section 4(1) of
the Act;
"interim ASBO" means an interim ASBO under section 7(2) of the
Act;
"parenting order" means a parenting order under section 13 or 102 of
the Act; and
"the Principal Reporter" means the Principal Reporter appointed
under section 127 of the Local Government etc. (Scotland) Act
1994.

(2) Any reference to a section shall, unless the context otherwise
requires, be a reference to a section of the Act.

**Applications for variation or revocation of ASBOs to be made by
minute in the original process**
3.27.2.—(1) An application under section 5 (variation and revocation
of antisocial behaviour orders) shall be made by minute in the original
process of the application for the ASBO in relation to which the
variation or revocation is sought.

(2) Where the person subject to the ASBO is a child, a written
statement containing the views of the Principal Reporter on the
application referred to in rule 3.27.2(1) shall, where practicable, be
lodged with that application.

Application for an interim ASBO
3.27.3.—(1) An application for an interim ASBO shall be made by
crave in the initial writ in which an ASBO is sought.

(2) An application for an interim ASBO once craved shall be
moved to that effect.

(3) The sheriff shall not consider an application for an interim
ASBO until after the initial writ has been intimated to the person in
respect of whom that application is made and, where that person is a
child, a written statement containing the views of the Principal
Reporter on that application has been lodged.

Notification of making etc. of ASBOs and interim ASBOs
3.27.4.—(1) Where a person is present in court at the time an ASBO
or interim ASBO is made or an ASBO to which that person is subject
is varied, service of a copy of the order making the ASBO or interim
ASBO or varying the ASBO, as the case may be, shall be made under
section 8(5)(a) or (b) and may be effected by the sheriff clerk—
  (a) giving such copy to and obtaining a receipt therefor from that
      person; or
  (b) sending such copy to that person by recorded delivery letter or
      registered post.

(2) Where a person is not present in court at the time an ASBO or
interim ASBO is made or an ASBO to which that person is subject is
varied, service of a copy of the order making the ASBO or interim
ASBO or varying the ASBO, as the case may be, shall be made under
section 8(5)(b) and shall be effected by such copy being sent to the
person subject to the ASBO or interim ASBO by recorded delivery
letter or registered post.

Parenting orders
3.27.5.—(1) Where a sheriff is considering making a parenting order
under section 13 (sheriff's power to make parenting order), the sheriff
shall order the applicant for the ASBO to—

   (a) intimate to any parent in respect of whom the parenting order is being considered—
      (i) that the court is considering making a parenting order in respect of that parent;
      (ii) that if that parent wishes to oppose the making of such a parenting order, he or she may attend or be represented at the hearing at which the sheriff considers the making of the parenting order;
      (iii) the place, date and time of the hearing set out in sub—paragraph (a)(ii) above; and
      (iv) that if that parent fails to appear and is not represented at the hearing, a parenting order may be made in respect of the parent; and
   (b) serve on any parent in respect of whom the parenting order is being considered a copy of the initial writ in which the ASBO is sought.

(2) Any parent in respect of whom a parenting order under section 13 is being considered may be sisted as a party to the action on their own motion, on the motion of either party or by the sheriff of his own motion.

Closure notice

3.27.6.—(1) A closure notice served under section 27 (service etc.) shall be in the form of Form 25 and shall (in addition to the requirements set out in section 27(5))—
   (a) state that it has been authorised by a senior police officer;
   (b) specify the date, time and place of the hearing of the application for a closure order under section 28; and
   (c) state that any person living on or having control of, responsibility for or an interest in the premises to which the closure notice relates who wishes to oppose the application should attend or be represented.

(2) Certification of service of a copy of the closure notice to all persons identified in accordance with section 27(2)(b) shall be in the form of Form 26.

Application for closure orders

3.27.7. An application to the sheriff for a closure order under section 28 shall be in the form of Form 27.

Application for extension of closure orders

3.27.8. An application to the sheriff for an extension of a closure order under section 32 shall be by minute in the form of Form 28 lodged in the original process of the application for the closure order in relation to which the extension is sought and shall be lodged not less than 21 days before the closure order to which it relates is due to expire.

Application for revocation of closure order

3.27.9. An application to the sheriff for revocation of a closure order under section 33 shall be by minute in the form of Form 29 lodged in the original process of the application for the closure order in relation to which the revocation is sought.

Application for access to premises

3.27.10. An application to the sheriff for an order for access to premises under section 34 shall be by minute in the form of Form 30 lodged in the original process of the application for the closure order in relation to which the access order is sought.

Applications by summary application
3.27.11. An application under section 35 (Reimbursement of expenditure), 63 (Appeal against graffiti removal notice) or 64 (Appeal against notice under section 61(4)) shall be by summary application.
3.27.12. An application under section 71 (Failure to comply with notice: order as to rental income), 74 (Failure to comply with notice: management control order) or 97 (Appeals against notice under section 94) shall be by summary application.

Revocation and suspension of order as to rental income
3.27.13. An application under section 73(2) for the revocation or suspension of an order relating to rental income shall be by minute lodged in the original process of the application for the order relating to rental income in relation to which the order for revocation or suspension is sought.

Revocation of management control order
3.27.14. An application under section 76(1) for the revocation of a management control order shall be by minute lodged in the original process of the application for the management control order in relation to which the order for revocation is sought.

Review of parenting order
3.27.15.—(1) An application under section 105(1) for revocation or variation of a parenting order shall be by minute lodged in the original process of the application for the parenting order in relation to which the order for revocation or variation is sought.

(2) Where the court that made a parenting order makes an order under section 105(5) that court shall within 4 days transmit the original process relating to the parenting order to the court specified in that order.

Procedural requirements relating to parenting orders
3.27.16. Where the sheriff is considering making a parenting order, or a revocation or variation of a parenting order, and it is practicable, having regard to the age and maturity of the child to—
(a) give the child an opportunity to indicate whether the child wishes to express views; and
(b) if the child so wishes, give the child an opportunity to express those views,
the sheriff shall order intimation in the form of Form 31 to the child in respect of whom the order was or is proposed to be made.
3.27.17. Where the sheriff is considering making a parenting order or revoking or varying a parenting order and does not already have sufficient information about the child, the sheriff shall order intimation in the form of Form 32 to the local authority for the area in which the child resides.

Enforcement of local authorities' duties under section 71 of the Children (Scotland) Act 1995
3.27.18. An application under section 71A(2) of the Children (Scotland) Act 1995 by the Principal Reporter shall be by summary

application to the sheriff principal of the Sheriffdom in which the principal office of the local authority is situated.".

(5) In Schedule 1 (Forms), after Form 24 insert Forms 25 to 32 as set out in the Schedule to this Act of Sederunt.

SCHEDULE

Article 2(5)

FORM 25

Rule 3.27.6(1)

Antisocial Behaviour etc. (Scotland) Act 2004

CLOSURE NOTICE

Section 27

1. The service of this closure notice is authorised by a senior police officer under section 26(1) of the Antisocial Behaviour etc. (Scotland) Act 2004 ("the Act").

2. The premises to which this closure notice relates are: *(specify premises)*.

3. Access to those premises by any person other than—
    (a) a person who habitually resides in the premises; or
    (b) the owner of the premises,
      is prohibited.

4. Failure to comply with this notice is an offence which may result in a fine of up to £2,500 or imprisonment for a term of up to 3 months (or both). The penalties may be higher for repeated failure to comply with this (or any other) closure notice.

5. An application for the closure of these premises will be made under section 28 of the Act and will be considered at *(insert place including Room No. if appropriate)* on the [ ] day of [ ] at [ ] am/pm.

6. On such an application as set out in paragraph 5 being made, the sheriff may make a closure order under section 29 of the Act in respect of these premises.

7. The effect of the Closure Order in respect of these premises would be to close the premises to all persons (other than any person expressly authorised access by the sheriff in terms of section 29(3) of the Act) for such period not exceeding 3 months as is specified in the order. Measures may be taken to ensure that the premises are securely closed against entry by any person.

8. If you live on or have control of, responsibility for or an interest in the premises to which this closure notice relates and wish to oppose the application for a closure order, you should attend or be represented at the hearing mentioned in paragraph 5 of this notice.

9. If you would like further information or advice about housing or legal matters you can contact—
(specify at least two persons or organisations (including name and means of contacting) based in the locality of the promises who or which will be able to provide advice about housing and legal matters). You also have a legal right to advice from your local authority should you be threatened with possible homelessness.

FORM 26

Rule 3.27.6(2)

Antisocial Behaviour etc. (Scotland) Act 2004

CERTIFICATION OF SERVICE

Section 27

I *(insert designation, including address and rank, of police officer)* certify that a copy of the closure notice which was authorised by *(insert designation of senior police officer)* on *(insert date on which closure notice was authorised)* in respect of *(insert details of the premises to which closure notice relates)* was served on: *(insert name and address of each person to whom a copy of the notice was given, including date)*

---

by *(insert designation, including address and rank, of police officer who served the copy or copies of the closure notice and, if more than one, indicate which police officer served a copy of the notice on which of the persons listed above).*

Signed

(insert designation, including rank, of police officer)

FORM 27

Rule 3.27.7

Antisocial Behaviour etc. (Scotland) Act 2004

Section 28

Sheriff Court .... 20.............

(Court Ref No.)

PART A

APPLICATION FOR CLOSURE ORDER IN RESPECT OF PREMISES AT:

("the Premises")

PART B

1. This application is made [by/on behalf of] *(delete as appropriate) (insert name and rank of senior police officer)* of *(insert details of police force).*

2. Service of a closure notice on the Premises was authorised by *(insert details of senior police officer)* on the [ ] day of [ ]. A copy of [the authorisation/written confirmation of such authorisation] *(delete as appropriate)* is attached.

3. A copy of the closure notice was, on the [ ] day of [ ],—
    (a) fixed to:
        (insert details of all locations in, or used as part of, the Premises, to which a copy of the notice was fixed)

_____

_____

_____

; and

(b) given to:
(insert name and address of each person to whom a copy of the notice was given)

_____

_____

_____

_____

_____

4. Certification in the prescribed form of service of the closure notice to the persons described at paragraph 3(b) above is attached.

5. This application is made on the following grounds:
(insert reasons for making application)

_____

_____

_____

_____

6. The following evidence is [attached/supplied] *(delete as appropriate)* in respect of this application *(insert short details of supporting evidence)*.

PART C

7. The applicant asks the court to—
    (a) assign the hearing for the [] day of [] at [] am/pm; and
    (b) make a closure order in respect of the Premises.

.... Signed
Senior Police Officer for [Police Force] (Applicant)
or [X.Y.] Solicitor for Senior Police Officer
(add designation and business address)

FORM OF INTERLOCUTOR

Sheriff Court .... 20................

(Court Ref No.)

The sheriff having considered this application assigns .... at .... within .... as a hearing, this date having been previously intimated to known interested persons and published in the closure notice.

.... Signed

Sheriff

FORM OF INTERLOCUTOR

Sheriff Court .... 20 ....

(Court Ref No.)

The sheriff having heard *(insert details of parties who attended the hearing)* and having considered the application [, being satisfied that the conditions mentioned in section 30(2) of the Antisocial Behaviour etc. (Scotland) Act 2004 are met] *(delete as appropriate)* and having regard to the matters mentioned in section 30(3) of the Antisocial Behaviour etc. (Scotland) Act 2004 ("the Act"),

*1. makes an order under section 29(1) of the Act that the premises at *(insert details of premises)* are closed to all persons for a period of *(insert period)*.

*2. directs intimation of this interlocutor to *(insert details of all known interested persons)* and by posting a copy thereof at prominent places on the premises at *(indicate where copies have been posted)*.

*3. refuses to make a closure order in respect of the premises at *(insert details of premises)*.

*4. postpones the determination of the application until *(insert date)* at *(insert time)* within *(insert location)*.

*delete as appropriate

.... Signed

Sheriff

FORM 28

Rule 3.27.8

Antisocial Behaviour etc. (Scotland) Act 2004

Minute

Section 32

Application for extension of closure order

Sheriff Court ....: .... 20.............

(Court Ref No.)

PART A

PREMISES IN RESPECT OF WHICH CLOSURE ORDER HAS BEEN MADE:

_____

_____

_____

("the Premises")

PART B

1. This application is made [by/on behalf of] *(delete as appropriate)* *(insert name and rank of senior police officer)* of *(insert details of police force)*.

2. A copy of the closure order made in respect of the Premises is attached. The closure order has effect until *(enter date)*.

3. The applicant believes that it is necessary to extend the period for which the closure order has effect for the purpose of preventing relevant harm, on the following grounds: *(specify reasons for extension)*.

4. *(Insert details of local authority)* has been consulted about the applicant's intention to make this application.

PART C

5. The applicant asks the court to—
   (c)   fix a hearing;
   (d)   order the applicant to intimate this application and the date of the hearing to such persons as the sheriff considers appropriate; and(e) extend the closure order in respect of the Premises for a period of [   ] [months/days] *(delete as appropriate)* or for such period not exceeding 6 months as the court may consider appropriate.

.... Signed

Senior Police Officer for [Police Force] (Applicant)

or [X.Y.] Solicitor for Senior Police Officer
(add designation and business address)

FORM OF INTERLOCUTOR

Sheriff Court .... 20.............

(Court Ref No.)

The sheriff having considered this minute orders the applicant to intimate this application and interlocutor to ...., assigns .... at .... within .... as a hearing and directs any person wishing to oppose the granting of the application to appear or be represented at the hearing to show cause why the application should not be granted.

.... Signed
Sheriff

FORM OF INTERLOCUTOR

Sheriff Court .... 20.............

(Court Ref No.)

The sheriff having heard *(insert details of parties who attended the hearing)* [and] having considered this minute [and being satisfied that the condition mentioned in section 32(1) of the Antisocial Behaviour etc. (Scotland) Act 2004 is met] *(delete as appropriate)*,

*1. makes an order extending the closure order made under section 29(1) of the Antisocial Behaviour etc. (Scotland) Act 2004 in respect of the premises at *(insert details of premises)* for a period of *(insert period)*.

*2. directs intimation of this interlocutor to *(insert details of persons to whom sheriff considers it to be appropriate to intimate)* and by posting a copy thereof at prominent places on the premises at *(indicate where copies have been posted)*.

*3. refuses to make an order extending the closure order in respect of the premises at *(insert details of premises)*.

*4. postpones the determination of the application until *(insert date)* at *(insert time)* within *(insert location)*.

*delete as appropriate.

.... Signed

Sheriff

FORM 29

Rule 3.27.9

Antisocial Behaviour etc. (Scotland) Act 2004

Minute

Section 33

Application for revocation of closure order

Sheriff Court .... 20............

(Court Ref No.)

PART A

PREMISES IN RESPECT OF WHICH CLOSURE ORDER HAS BEEN MADE:

_____

_____

_____

("the Premises")

The applicant is *(insert name and address of applicant)* who is:

*1. a senior police officer of the police force for the area within which the Premises (or part thereof) are situated.

*2. the local authority for the area within which the Premises or part thereof are situated.

*3. a person on whom a copy of the closure notice relating to the Premises in respect of which the closure order has effect was served under section 27(2)(b) or (3) of the Antisocial Behaviour etc. (Scotland) Act 2004.

*4. a person who has an interest in these premises but on whom the closure notice was not served.

*delete as appropriate.

PART B

1. A copy of the closure order made in respect of the Premises is attached.

2. The applicant believes that a closure order in respect of the Premises is no longer necessary to prevent the occurrence of relevant harm for the following reasons *(specify grounds for application for revocation)*.

PART C

3. The applicant asks the court to:
    (a) fix a hearing;
    (b) order the applicant to intimate this application and the date of the hearing to such persons as the sheriff considers appropriate and, where the applicant is not a senior police officer, to such senior police officer as the sheriff considers appropriate; and
    (c) order the revocation of the closure order.

.... Signed

Applicant *(include full designation)*
or [X.Y.] Solicitor for Applicant *(include full designation and business address)*

FORM OF INTERLOCUTOR

Sheriff Court .... 20............

(Court Ref No.)

The sheriff having considered this minute orders the applicant to intimate this application and interlocutor to ...., assigns .... within .... as a hearing and directs any person wishing to oppose the granting of the application to appear or be represented at the hearing to show cause why the application should not be granted.

.... Signed
Sheriff

FORM OF INTERLOCUTOR

Sheriff Court .... 20............

Act of Sederunt (SSI 2004/455)

(Court Ref No.)

The sheriff having heard *(insert details of parties who attended the hearing)* [and] having considered this minute [and being satisfied that a closure order is no longer necessary to prevent the occurrence of relevant harm] *(delete as appropriate)*,

*1. makes an order revoking the closure order made under section 29(1) of the Antisocial Behaviour etc. (Scotland) Act 2004 in respect of the premises at *(insert details of the premises)*.

*2. directs intimation of this interlocutor to *(insert details of persons to whom sheriff considers it to be appropriate to intimate)*.

*3. refuses to make an order revoking the closure order in respect of the premises at *(insert details of the premises)*.

*4. postpones the determination of the application until *(insert date)* at *(insert time)* within *(insert location)*.

*delete as appropriate

.... Signed
Sheriff

FORM 30

Rule 3.27.10

Antisocial Behaviour etc. (Scotland) Act 2004

Minute

Section 34

Application for access to premises in respect of which a closure order is in force

Sheriff Court .... 20.............

(Court Ref No.)

PART A

PREMISES IN RESPECT OF WHICH CLOSURE ORDER HAS BEEN MADE:

_____

_____

_____

("the Premises")

PREMISES IN RESPECT OF WHICH APPLICATION FOR ACCESS IS BEING MADE:

_____

_____

_____

PART B

1. A copy of the closure order made in respect of the Premises is attached. The closure order has effect until *(insert date)*.

2. The applicant *(insert details of applicant)* [owns/occupies] *(delete as appropriate)* the following [part of] *(delete as appropriate)* building or structure in which the Premises are situated and in respect of which the closure order does not have effect.

133

PART C

3. The applicant asks the court to:
   (a) fix a hearing;
   (b) order the applicant to intimate this application and the date of the hearing to such persons as the sheriff considers appropriate and, where the applicant is not a senior police officer, to such senior police officer as the sheriff considers appropriate; and(c) make an order allowing access *(detail access provisions requested)*.

.... Signed

Applicant *(include full designation)*

or [X.Y.] Solicitor for Applicant *(include full designation and business address)*

FORM OF INTERLOCUTOR

Sheriff Court .... 20............

(Court Ref No.)

The sheriff having considered this minute orders the applicant to intimate this application and interlocutor to ...., assigns .... at .... within .... as a hearing and directs any person wishing to oppose the granting of the application to appear or be represented at the hearing to show cause why the application should not be granted.

.... Signed

Sheriff

FORM OF INTERLOCUTOR

Sheriff Court .... 20............

(Court Ref No.)

The sheriff having heard *(insert details of parties who attended the hearing)* and having considered this minute,

*1. makes an order an order allowing *(insert name and address)*

———————————————————————————

———————————————————————————

access to the following part or parts of the premises at *(insert details of premises)* in relation to which a closure order has been made under section 29(1) of the Antisocial Behaviour etc. (Scotland) Act 2004: *(insert details of parts of premises to which access order is to apply)*

———————————————————————————

———————————————————————————

———————————————————————————

*2. directs intimation of this interlocutor to *(insert details of all known interested persons to whom the sheriff considers it to be appropriate to intimate)*.

*3. refuses to make an access order in respect of the premises at *(insert details of premises)*.

*4. postpones the determination of the application until *(insert date)* at *(insert time)* within *(insert location)*.

*delete as appropriate

.... Signed

Sheriff

FORM 31

Rule 3.27.16

Antisocial Behaviour etc. (Scotland) Act 2004

Section 13, 102 or 105

Intimation that court may make or revoke or vary a parenting order

Sheriff Court .... 20.............

(Court Ref No.)

PART A

This part must be completed by the applicant's solicitor in language a child is capable of understanding

To **(1)**

The Sheriff (the person who has to decide about the parenting order) has been asked by (2) to decide:—
  (a) **(3)** and **(4)**;
  (b) **(5)**;
  (c) **(6)**.

If you want to tell the Sheriff what you think about the things **(2)** has asked the Sheriff to decide about your future you should complete Part B of this form and send it to the Sheriff Clerk at **(7)** by **(8)**. An envelope which does not need a postage stamp is enclosed for you to use to return the form.

IF YOU DO NOT UNDERSTAND THIS FORM OR IF YOU WANT HELP TO COMPLETE IT you may get free help from a SOLICITOR or contact the SCOTTISH CHILD LAW CENTRE ON the FREE ADVICE TELEPHONE LINE ON 0800 328 8970.

If you return the form it will be given to the Sheriff. The Sheriff may wish to speak with you and may ask you to come and see him or her.

NOTES FOR COMPLETION

(1) Insert name and address of child.	(2) Insert description of party making the application to the court.
(3) Insert appropriate wording for parenting order sought.	(4) Insert appropriate wording, if relevant, for Antisocial Behaviour Order.
(5) Insert appropriate wording for contact.	(6) Insert appropriate wording for any other order sought or determinations to be made by sheriff.
(7) Insert address of sheriff clerk.	(8) Insert the date occurring 21 days after the date on which intimation is given.
(9) Insert court reference number.	(10) Insert name and address of parties to the action.

PART B

IF YOU WISH THE SHERIFF TO KNOW YOUR VIEWS ABOUT THE PARENTING ORDER YOU SHOULD COMPLETE THIS PART OF THE FORM

To the Sheriff Clerk, **(7)**

Court Ref. No. **(9)**

(10) ....

QUESTION (1): DO YOU WISH THE SHERIFF TO KNOW WHAT YOUR VIEWS ARE ABOUT THE PARENTING ORDER?

(PLEASE TICK BOX)

YES	
NO	

If you have ticked YES please also answer Question (2) *or* (3)

QUESTION (2): WOULD YOU LIKE A FRIEND, RELATIVE OR OTHER PERSON TO TELL THE SHERIFF YOUR VIEWS ABOUT THE PARENTING ORDER?

(PLEASE TICK BOX)

YES	
NO	

If you have ticked YES please write the name and address of the person you wish to tell the Sheriff your views in Box (A) below. You should also tell that person what your views are about the parenting order.

BOX A:	(NAME)				
	(ADDRESS)				
	Is this person—	A friend?		A teacher?	
		A relative?		Other?	

OR

QUESTION (3): WOULD YOU LIKE TO WRITE TO THE SHERIFF AND TELL HIM WHAT YOUR VIEWS ARE ABOUT THE PARENTING ORDER?

(PLEASE TICK BOX)

YES	
NO	

If you decide that you wish to write to the Sheriff you can write what your views are about the parenting order in Box (B) below or on a separate piece of paper. If you decide to write your views on a separate piece of paper you should send it along with this form to the Sheriff Clerk in the envelope provided.

BOX B:	WHAT I HAVE TO SAY ABOUT THE PARENTING ORDER:—

NAME: ....
ADDRESS: ....
DATE: ....

FORM 32

Rule 3.27.17

Antisocial Behaviour etc. (Scotland) Act 2004

Section 13, 102 or 105

Form of notice to local authority requesting a report in respect of a child

Sheriff Court .... 20.............

(Court Ref No.)

To *(insert name and address)*

1. YOU ARE GIVEN NOTICE that in an action in the Sheriff Court at *(insert address)* an application for [the variation/revocation of] *(delete as appropriate)* a parenting order is being considered in respect of a parent of the child *(insert name of child)*. A copy of the application is enclosed.

2. You are required to submit to the court a report on all the circumstances of the child, including but not limited to:—

    (a) the current or proposed arrangements for the case and upbringing of the child;
    (b) information about the family circumstances of the parent; and
    (c) the likely effect of a parenting order on the family circumstances of the parent and the child.

3. This report should be sent to the Sheriff Court at .... on or before .... *(insert date)*.

Date *(insert date)*

.... Signed:
Applicant *(include full designation)*
or [X.Y.] Solicitor for Applicant *(include full designation and business address)*
or Sheriff Clerk

ACT OF ADJOURNAL (CRIMINAL PROCEDURE RULES AMENDMENT NO. 5) (MISCELLANEOUS) 2004

(SSI 2004/481)

Made   *5th November 2004*
Coming into force   *26th November 2004*

The Lord Justice General, the Lord Justice Clerk and the Lords Commissioners of Justiciary, under and by virtue of the powers conferred on them by section 305 of the Criminal Procedure (Scotland) Act 1995, and of all other powers enabling them in that behalf, do hereby enact and declare:

Citation and commencement
1.—(1) This Act of Adjournal may be cited as the Act of Adjournal (Criminal Procedure Rules Amendment No. 5) (Miscellaneous) 2004 and shall come into force on 26th November 2004.

(2) This Act of Adjournal shall be inserted in the Books of Adjournal.

Amendment of the Act of Adjournal (Criminal Procedure Rules) 1996
2.—(1) The Act of Adjournal (Criminal Procedure Rules) 1996 hall be amended in accordance with the following sub-paragraphs.

(2) In rule 8A.2(1) (further pre-trial diet) for "72F(3)" there shall be substituted "72F(5)".

(3) In rule 13A.1 (citation of witnesses for precognition) for "of this Act" there shall be substituted "of the Act".

(4) After rule 20.19 (reduction of disqualification period for drink-drive offenders) there shall be inserted the following:—

> **"Antisocial behaviour orders**
> **20.20.** An antisocial behaviour order made under section 234AA of the Act of 1995(c) shall be in Form 20.20.".

(5) After Chapter 46 (parental directions under the Sexual Offences Act 2003), there shall be inserted the following:—

"CHAPTER 47

PROTECTION OF CHILDREN (SCOTLAND) ACT 2003

References under the Protection of Children (Scotland) Act 2003
47.1. Where section 10(5) of the Protection of Children (Scotland) Act 2003 applies, the clerk of court shall forthwith—
(a) post a notice of reference in Form 47.1; and
(b) transmit, by facsimile or other electronic means, a copy of that notice,
to the Scottish Ministers.".

(6) In the appendix—
(a) in the heading for Form 13A.1—A (form of citation of witness for precognition) for "Form 13A.1—A" there shall be substituted "Form 13A.1";
(b) after Form 20.19–B there shall be inserted the form set out in Part 1 of the Schedule to this Act of Adjournal;

(c) at the end there shall be inserted the form set out in Part 2 of the Schedule to this Act of Adjournal.

SCHEDULE

PART 1

Paragraph 2(4)

Form 20.20

Rule 20.20

Form of antisocial behaviour order under section 234AA of the Criminal Procedure (Scotland) Act 1995

ANTISOCIAL BEHAVIOUR ORDER

under section 234AA of the Criminal Procedure (Scotland) Act 1995

COURT:

DATE:

OFFENDER:

Address:

Date of Birth:

THE COURT, being satisfied under section 234AA(2)(d) that the making of an antisocial behaviour order is necessary;

AND the court having explained to the offender the effect of this order (including the requirements set out below) and that if he or she, without reasonable excuse, does anything that the order to which he or she is subject prohibits him or her from doing, shall be guilty of an offence, and that the court has the power to revoke or vary the order on the application of the offender subject to the order;

ORDERS that the offender shall for (*specify period*) from the date of this order be prohibited from (*specify prohibitions imposed*)

(i)

(ii)

(iii)

(*Signed*)

Clerk of Court

Copy: Offender

Local Authority.

PART 2

Paragraph 2(5)

Form 47.1

Rule 47.1

Form of notice of reference under section 10(5) of the Protection of Children (Scotland) Act 2003

Reference number: (*specify*)

To: The Scottish Ministers

TAKE NOTICE that the case of the individual named below is referred to you by the court under section 10(5) of the Protection of Children (Scotland) Act 2003.

That is because—
- BY the individual named below has been convicted of an offence against a child;
- on convicting that individual, the court proposed to refer the case of that individual to you, the Scottish Ministers; and
- either—
    - (a) the period during which an appeal against that proposed reference might have been brought has expired without an appeal being brought; or
    - (b) an appeal against the proposed reference was brought within that period but the appeal has now been dismissed or abandoned.

Name of individual: (*name and any known aliases*)

Address: (*specify last known address*)

Date of birth: (*date*)

Court: (*specify*)

Date of conviction: (*date*)

Offence(s): (*specify*)

Date of offence(s): (*date*)

(*Signed*)

Depute Clerk of Justiciary [*or* Sheriff Clerk Depute]

Date: (*date*)

Telephone number: (*specify*)

E—mail address: (*specify*)

THE COMMUNITY REPARATION ORDERS (REQUIREMENTS FOR CONSULTATION AND PRESCRIBED ACTIVITIES) (SCOTLAND) REGULATIONS 2005

(SSI 2005/18)

Made	*18th January 2005*
Laid before the Scottish Parliament	*19th January 2005*
Coming into force	*10th February 2005*

The Scottish Ministers, in exercise of the powers conferred by section 27(5A) of the Social Work (Scotland) Act 1968, section 245K(5) of the Criminal Procedure (Scotland) Act 1995 and section 141(2)(a) of the Antisocial Behaviour etc. (Scotland) Act 2004 and of all other powers enabling them in that behalf, hereby make the following Regulations:

Citation and commencement
1. These Regulations may be cited as the Community Reparation Orders (Requirements for Consultation and Prescribed Activities) (Scotland) Regulations 2005 and shall come into force on 10th February 2005.

Provision for Persons subject to Community Reparation Orders
2. The following persons and classes of person are prescribed for the purposes of section 27(5A) of the Social Work (Scotland) Act 1968:—
    (a) the Chief Constable for the area of the local authority making, revising or modifying the community justice scheme;
    (b) such organisations representative of communities in the local authority's area as the local authority thinks appropriate;
    (c) such organisations representative of victims of crime as the local authority thinks appropriate;
    (d) such organisations representative of commercial and retail businesses operating in the local authority's area as the local authority thinks appropriate;
    (e) any Community Safety Partnership led by the local authority;
    (f) leaders of such groups representing ethnic minorities within the local authority's area as the local authority thinks appropriate; and
    (g) as regards offenders under the age of 16 years, such individuals and organisations representing the interests of young people as the local authority thinks appropriate.

Prescribed activities
3. The following activities are prescribed for the purposes of section 245K(5) of the Criminal Procedure (Scotland) Act 1995—
    (a) unpaid work that, in the view of the supervising officer appointed by the local authority, the offender is capable of undertaking that will enable reparation to be made in accordance with section 245K(5)(a) of that Act;
    (b) programmes designed to increase the awareness of offenders of the effect that anti social behaviour has on the victims of such behaviour and on the local community more generally;

(c) programmes designed to reduce future offending and instances of anti social behaviour;

(d) programmes designed to encourage personal and social responsibility on the part of offenders and the development of appropriate life skills.

THE ANTISOCIAL BEHAVIOUR (NOISE CONTROL) (SCOTLAND) REGULATIONS 2005

(SSI 2005/43)

Made	*27th January 2005*
Laid before the Scottish Parliament	*28th January 2005*
Coming into force	*28th February 2005*

The Scottish Ministers, in exercise of the powers conferred by sections 48, 49 and 141(2)(a) and (b) of the Antisocial Behaviour etc. (Scotland) Act 2004, and of all other powers enabling them in that behalf, hereby make the following Regulations:

Citation and commencement
1. These Regulations may be cited as the Antisocial Behaviour (Noise Control) (Scotland) Regulations 2005 and shall come into force on 28th February 2005.

Interpretation
2.—(1) In these Regulations:
"the Act" means the Antisocial Behaviour etc. (Scotland) Act 2004;
"approved device" means a device approved under regulation 4 or 5;
"A-weighted sound pressure level" means the A-weighted sound pressure level in decibels calculated in accordance with the formula set out in paragraph 3.3 of BS 7445;
"BS 7445" means the British Standard entitled "Description and measurement of environmental noise—Part 1: Guide to quantities and procedures", published by the British Standards Institution and numbered BS 7445–1: 2003;
"BS 7580" means the British Standard entitled "Specification for the verification of sound level meters—Part 1 Comprehensive Procedure", published by the British Standards Institution and numbered BS 7580: Part 1: 1997;
"BS EN 60942" means the British Standard entitled "Electroacoustics—Sound calibrators", published by the British Standards Institution and numbered BS EN 60942: 2003;
"BS EN 61672" means the British Standard entitled "Electroacoustics—sound level meters—Part 1: Specifications", published by the British Standards Institution and numbered BS EN 61672–1: 2003;
"EEA State" means a Member State, Norway, Iceland or Liechtenstein;
"equivalent continuous A-weighted sound pressure level" means the equivalent continuous A-weighted sound pressure level in decibels, calculated in accordance with the formula set out in paragraph 3.5 of BS 7445;
"$L_{AN,T}$" means the measurement of the A-weighted sound pressure level, calculated in accordance with paragraph 3.4 of BS 7445;
"sound calibrator" has the meaning given in paragraph 3.1 of BS EN 60942 and for the purposes of regulation 8 a sound calibrator must comply with the requirements of Class 1 of that standard;
"time-weighting" has the meaning given in paragraph 3.4 of BS EN 61672 and for the purposes of these Regulations time-weighting 'F' is calculated using a specified time constant of 0.125 seconds;
"underlying level of noise" means the level of ambient noise expressed in decibels and measured by an approved device used in accordance with the provisions of regulation 7.

(1) In these Regulations, any reference to a British Standard shall include a reference to:
- (a) a relevant standard or code of practice of a national standards body or equivalent body of any EEA State or of Turkey;
- (b) any relevant international standard recognised for use as a standard by any EEA State or of Turkey; or
- (c) a technical specification or code of practice which, whether mandatory or not, is recognised for use as a standard by a public authority of any EEA State or of Turkey,

   in so far as the standard, code of practice, international standard or technical specification in question enables the objectives of these Regulations to be met in an equivalent manner.

Permitted levels
3. For the purposes of section 48 of the Act (permitted level of noise), the permitted levels prescribed in Column 2 of the Schedule to these Regulations may be emitted from relevant property during the periods prescribed in the corresponding entry in Column 1 of that Schedule.

Approved measuring devices—noise emitted from relevant property
4. For the purposes of section 49(1) of the Act (approval of measuring devices) sound level meters which comply with the requirements of Class 1 of BS EN 61672 are devices approved for the measurement of noise emitted from relevant property, when used in accordance with the requirements of regulations 6 and 8.

Approved measuring devices—underlying level of noise
5.—(1) For the purposes of section 49(1) of the Act (approval of measuring devices), subject to paragraph (2), sound level meters which:
- (a) comply with the requirements of Class 1 of BS EN 61672; and
- (b) are capable of determining the A-weighted sound pressure level using time-weighting 'F',

are devices approved for the measurement of the underlying level of noise, when used in accordance with the requirements of regulations 7 and 8.

(2) Where $L_{AN,T}$ measurements are used to determine the underlying level of noise, the devices specified in paragraph (1) must in addition:
- (a) sample the sound pressure level at a rate of not less than 10 times per second; and
- (b) use in the statistical calculation a class interval of no greater than 0.5 decibels.

(3) When time weighting 'F' is used for the purposes of paragraph (1) it shall not exceed 0.6 seconds in a period of no shorter than one minute and no longer than 5 minutes.

Measurement of noise emitted from relevant property
6.—(1) The provisions of this regulation shall apply when a device is used to measure noise emitted from relevant property.

(2) If the measurement of noise is made within a room in the relevant place, the windows and doors in that room shall be closed.

(3) The measuring microphone of the approved device shall be positioned at least 0.5 metres away from any surface in the room (including the floor) and from any items of furniture.

(4) Within a period of no more than 15 minutes beginning with the time at which the measurement of noise is made, the equivalent continuous A-weighted sound pressure level of the noise emitted from the relevant

property shall be measured for a period of 5 minutes, except where pauses are required to exclude from the measurement any significant noise other than the noise causing complaint.

(5) Where the measurement obtained under paragraph (4) is not a whole number, it shall be rounded down to the nearest whole number.

Measurement of the underlying level of noise
7.—(1) The provisions of this regulation shall apply when a device is used to measure the underlying level of noise.

(2) If the measurement is made within a room in the relevant place, the windows and doors in that room shall be closed.

(3) The measuring microphone of the approved device shall be positioned at least 0.5 metres away from any surface in the room (including the floor) and from any items of furniture.

(4) The A-weighted sound pressure level shall be measured using time-weighting 'F'.

(5) Where a measurement obtained under paragraph (4) is not a whole number, it shall be rounded up to the nearest whole number.

(6) The measurement under paragraph (4) shall be made at the same time as the measurement under regulation 6(4).

Verification and testing of approved devices
8.—(1) The sensitivity of a device approved under regulation 4 or 5 must be verified before and after its use, using a sound calibrator.

(2) Where—
(a) the sensitivity of the device has been verified after the measurement of noise in accordance with paragraph (1); and (b) the sensitivity level of the device has changed by 0.5 decibels or more from the level indicated when the sensitivity of the device was verified before the measurement of noise,
that measurement may not be used for any of the purposes set out in these Regulations.

(3) A device approved under regulation 4 or 5 and the sound calibrator used in relation to it, must be tested in accordance with the requirements of BS 7580—
(a) no more than 2 years before it is used for any of the purposes set out in these Regulations; and
(b) at least once every 2 years following that test.

SCHEDULE

Regulation 3

PERMITTED LEVELS

Column 1	Column 2
Periods of the day	*Permitted level*
7 am to 7 pm in any day	41 decibels, where the underlying level of noise does not exceed 31 decibels; or where the underlying level of noise exceeds 31 decibels, 10 decibels in excess of that underlying level of noise.
7 pm to 11 pm in any day	37 decibels, where the underlying level of noise does not exceed 27 decibels; or where the underlying level of noise exceeds 27 decibels, 10 decibels in excess of that underlying level of noise.

Column 1	Column 2
Periods of the day	*Permitted level*
11 pm on any day to 7 am in the following day	31 decibels, where the underlying level of noise does not exceed 21 decibels; or where the underlying level of noise exceeds 21 decibels, 10 decibels in excess of that underlying level of noise.

THE POLICE (RETENTION AND DISPOSAL OF MOTOR VEHICLES) (SCOTLAND) REGULATIONS 2005

(SSI 2005/80)

Made	*22nd February 2005*
Laid before Parliament	*23rd February 2005*
Coming into force	*17th March 2005*

The Scottish Ministers, in exercise of the powers conferred on them by section 127 of the Antisocial Behaviour etc. (Scotland) Act 2004 and of all other powers enabling them in that behalf, hereby make the following Regulations:

Citation and commencement
1. These Regulations may be cited as the Police (Retention and Disposal of Motor Vehicles) (Scotland) Regulations 2005 and shall come into force on 17th March 2005.

Interpretation
2. In these Regulations—
   "the 2004 Act" means the Antisocial Behaviour etc. (Scotland) Act 2004;
   "GB registration mark" means a registration mark issued in relation to a motor vehicle under the Vehicle Excise and Registration Act 1994;
   "motor vehicle" means any mechanically propelled vehicle, whether or not it is intended or adapted for use on roads;
   "owner" includes—
   (a) the person by whom, according to the records maintained by the Secretary of State in connection with any functions exercisable by him by virtue of the Vehicle Excise and Registration Act 1994, the motor vehicle is kept and used; or
   (b) in relation to a motor vehicle which is the subject of a hire agreement or a hire-purchase agreement, the person entitled to possession of the motor vehicle under the agreement;
   "relevant motor vehicle" means a motor vehicle which has been seized and removed under section 126(3)(b) of the 2004 Act;
   "the retaining authority" means a constable or such other person authorised by the chief constable under regulation 3(1);
   "seizure notice" means a notice complying with regulation 4;
   "specified information", in relation to a motor vehicle, means such of the following information as can be or could have been ascertained from an inspection of the motor vehicle, or has been ascertained from any other source, that is to say—
   (c) in the case of a motor vehicle which carries a GB registration mark, or a mark indicating registration in a place outside Great Britain, particulars of that mark; and
   (d) the make of the motor vehicle.

Retention and safe keeping of motor vehicles
3.—(1) A relevant motor vehicle shall be passed into and remain in the custody of a constable or other person authorised under this regulation by the chief constable of the police force for the area in which the motor vehicle is seized (the "retaining authority") until—
   (a) the retaining authority permits it to be removed from their custody by a person appearing to the retaining authority to be the owner of the motor vehicle; or

(b) it has been disposed of under these Regulations.

(2) Whilst any motor vehicle is in such custody, the retaining authority shall be under a duty to take such steps as are reasonably necessary for its safe keeping.

Giving of seizure notice

4.—(1) The retaining authority shall, as soon as possible after a relevant motor vehicle has been taken into their custody, take such steps as are practicable to give a seizure notice to the person who is or appears to be the owner of that motor vehicle, except where the motor vehicle has been released from their custody in accordance with these Regulations.

(2) A seizure notice required to be given under these Regulations shall comply with, and be given in accordance with, the following provisions of this regulation.

(3) A seizure notice shall, in respect of the motor vehicle to which it relates, contain the specified information and shall state—

(a) the place where the motor vehicle was seized;

(b) the police area where it is now being kept;

(c) that the person to whom the notice is directed is required to claim the motor vehicle from the retaining authority on or before the date specified in the notice, being a date not less than 7 days from the day when the notice is given to that person;

(d) that unless the motor vehicle is claimed on or before that date the retaining authority intends to dispose of it; and

(e) that, subject to regulation 5(3), charges are payable under these Regulations by the owner of the motor vehicle in respect of the removal and retention of the motor vehicle, and that the motor vehicle may be retained until such charges are paid.

(4) The seizure notice shall be given—

(a) by delivering it to the person to whom it is directed;

(b) by leaving it at that person's usual or last known address;

(c) by addressing it to that person and sending it by registered post to that person's usual or last known address;

(d) if the person is a body corporate, by delivering it to the secretary or clerk of the body at its registered or principal office, or sending it by registered post, addressed to the secretary or clerk of the body at that office; or

(e) if the person is a limited liability partnership or a member of the partnership, by sending it by registered post to the registered or principal office of the partnership.

Release of vehicles

5.—(1) Subject to the provisions of these Regulations, if, before a relevant motor vehicle is disposed of by a retaining authority, a person satisfies the retaining authority that they are the owner of that motor vehicle and pay to the retaining authority such a charge in respect of its removal and retention as is provided for in regulation 6, the retaining authority shall permit that person to remove the motor vehicle from such custody.

(2) In determining whether the retaining authority is satisfied that a person who claims to be the owner of a relevant motor vehicle is in fact the owner, the retaining authority may consider such documentary evidence as may be supplied.

(3) A person who would otherwise be liable to pay a charge under paragraph (1) shall not be liable to pay it if—

(a) the use by reference to which the motor vehicle was seized under section 126 of the 2004 Act was not a use by that person; and

(b) that person did not know of the use of the motor vehicle in the manner which led to its seizure, had not consented to its use in that manner and could not, by the taking of reasonable steps, have prevented its use in that manner.

Charges in relation to the removal and retention of a motor vehicle
6.—(1) The charge payable under regulation 5(1) shall be—
   (a) in respect of the motor vehicle's removal, £105; and
   (b) in respect of retention, £12 for each period of 24 hours or a part thereof during which the motor vehicle is in the custody of the retaining authority.

(2) For the purposes of paragraph (1)(b), each period of 24 hours shall be reckoned from noon on the first day after removal during which the place at which the motor vehicle is stored is open for the claiming of such motor vehicles before noon.

Disposal of motor vehicles
7.—(1) Where the retaining authority has been unable to give a seizure notice to the person who is or appears to be the owner of a relevant motor vehicle or, following the giving of such a seizure notice, the motor vehicle has not been released from the custody of the retaining authority under these Regulations, the retaining authority may dispose of the motor vehicle in accordance with the following provisions of this regulation.

(2) If the retaining authority is satisfied that the person to whom a seizure notice has been given is the owner of the motor vehicle, the retaining authority may dispose of the motor vehicle at any time, subject to paragraph (6).

(3) Where the retaining authority is not so satisfied, it may, after taking steps under paragraph (5) to find a person who may be the owner of the motor vehicle and any other steps for that purpose which appear to the retaining authority to be practicable, in such manner as the retaining authority thinks fit dispose of the motor vehicle at any time, subject to paragraph (6), if—
   (a) the retaining authority fails to find such a person, allowing a reasonable time for any person or body from whom the retaining authority has requested information to respond to the request; or
   (b) the retaining authority finds such a person but that person fails to comply with a seizure notice given under regulation 4; or
   (c) the retaining authority finds such a person but that person is someone to whom the retaining authority has already given a seizure notice under regulation 4.

(4) For the purpose of paragraphs (2) and (3)(c), the expression "given" in respect of service of a seizure notice includes an attempt to serve a seizure notice.

(5) The steps to be taken under this paragraph to find a person who may be the owner of the motor vehicle shall be such of the following as are applicable to the vehicle—
   (a) if the motor vehicle carries a GB registration mark—
      (i) the retaining authority shall ascertain from the records maintained by the Secretary of State in connection with any functions exercisable by him by virtue of the Vehicle Excise and Registration Act 1994 the name and address of the person by whom the motor vehicle is kept and used; and
      (ii) the retaining authority shall give, where practicable, the specified information to a relevant agency and shall enquire of them

whether they can make any enquiries to find the owner of the motor vehicle;

(b) if the motor vehicle carries a registration mark other than a GB registration mark, the retaining authority shall, where practicable, give the specified information to a relevant agency and shall enquire of them whether they can make any enquiries to find the owner of the motor vehicle.

(6) The retaining authority may not dispose of the motor vehicle under this regulation—

(a) during the period of 3 months starting with the date on which the motor vehicle was seized;

(b) if the period in sub-paragraph (a) has expired, until after the date specified by virtue of regulation 4(3)(c); or

(c) if not otherwise covered by sub-paragraph (a) or (b), during the period of 7 days starting with the date on which the motor vehicle is claimed under regulation 5.

(7) In this regulation, "relevant agency" means such agency maintaining records of hire purchase agreements about motor vehicles as the retaining authority considers appropriate.

Payment of proceeds of sale to owner of motor vehicle
8.—(1) Where the retaining authority disposes of a motor vehicle in pursuance of these Regulations by means of sale, the retaining authority shall pay the net proceeds of sale to any person who, before the end of the period of one year beginning with the date on which the motor vehicle is sold, satisfies the retaining authority that at the time of the sale they were the owner of the motor vehicle.

(2) If it appears to the retaining authority that more than one person is the owner of a particular motor vehicle, such one of them as the retaining authority thinks fit shall be treated as its owner for the purposes of paragraph (1).

(3) In this regulation, "the net proceeds of sale" means any sum by which the proceeds of sale exceed the aggregate of such sums as may be payable under these Regulations in respect of the removal and retention of the motor vehicle.

THE ANTISOCIAL BEHAVIOUR (FIXED PENALTY NOTICE) (ADDITIONAL INFORMATION) (SCOTLAND) ORDER 2005

(SSI 2005/130)

Made	*3rd March 2005*
Laid before the Scottish Parliament	*4th March 2005*
Coming into force	*1st April 2005*

The Scottish Ministers, in exercise of the powers conferred by section 130(3)(f) of the Antisocial Behaviour etc. (Scotland) Act 2004, and of all other powers enabling them in that behalf, hereby make the following Order:

Citation, commencement and interpretation
1.—(1) This Order may be cited as the Antisocial Behaviour (Fixed Penalty Notice)(Additional Information) (Scotland) Order 2005 and shall come into force on 1st April 2005.

(2) In this Order—

"fixed penalty notice" shall have the same meaning as section 129(2) of the Antisocial Behaviour etc. (Scotland) Act 2004.

Additional information to be included on a fixed penalty notice
2. For the purposes of section 130(3)(f) of the Antisocial etc. Behaviour (Scotland) Act 2004 a fixed penalty notice shall include the following other information:

(a) the name, address and date of birth of the person to whom the fixed penalty notice is given;

(b) the date and time on which the fixed penalty notice was given;

(c) the place at which the fixed penalty notice was given;

(d) the particulars of the constable who gave the fixed penalty notice;

(e) information connected with the administration of the fixed penalty notice; and

(f) the method of payment for the fixed penalty.

INDEX

155

Index